A DONKEY IN T

Derek Tangye has become famous all over the world for his series of best sellers about his flower farm in Cornwall. The series, which began with *A Gull On The Roof*, describes a simple way of life which thousands of his readers would like to adopt themselves.

Derek and his wife, Jeannie, left their glamorous existence in London when they discovered Minack, a deserted cottage close to the cliffs of Mount's Bay. Jeannie gave up her job as Press Relations Officer of the Savoy Hotel Group and Derek Tangye resigned from M.I.5. They then proceeded to carve from the wild land around the cottage the meadows which became their flower farm.

A Donkey in the Meadow

Derek Tangye

SPHERE BOOKS LIMITED
30-32 Gray's Inn Road, London WC1X 8JL

First published in Great Britain by Michael Joseph Ltd, 1965
Copyright © Derek Tangye 1965
Published by Sphere Books Ltd, 1980
Reprinted 1983

Text set in 10/11½ pt. Baskerville

Printed and bound in Great Britain by
Collins, Glasgow

To
Romilly

I

'When do we go?'

It was a sunny April morning, and we were sitting on the white seat beside the bare verbena bush eating our breakfast; a liner aslant from the Lizard on the horizon, Lama, the little black cat at our feet, and Boris, the muscovy drake, staring at us a few yards up the path.

'Have you really made up your mind?'

I knew what Jeannie was thinking. We had discussed holidays before. We had perused the map, had our passports renewed, thought about Brittany, decided on Paris, then changed our minds to London, and in the end had gone nowhere.

'Yes,' I said, 'you have persuaded me.'

A holiday sometimes begins as a course of duty. There are people, for instance, who have to be exploded out of their homes in order to escape to the enjoyment of a holiday. I am one of them.

'The point is,' Jeannie had said to me earlier, 'you haven't been away from Minack for eight years.'

'I haven't wanted to.'

'You've worked very hard all these years on the flower farm.'

'You too.'

'You've also written two books that in successive years were high up in the *Sunday Times* best seller list.'

'Flattery!'

'You've also sold one for a Walt Disney film.'

'What's all this leading up to?'

'It's time you saw one of your books in a London bookshop.'

7

'You're appealing to my vanity.'

'Seriously . . . I'm suggesting you see in their own surroundings the people you work with.'

'A business holiday.'

'If you like to put it that way. You would be able to wake up in the morning without having to worry about gales or what's made the tractor break down or what disease has hit the freesias . . . and concentrate on your other career.'

'And find out which is the more satisfying?'

'You can't deny,' said Jeannie, flinging a bacon rind at Boris, 'that things have been changing. I mean pressures have been put on us that remind us of the reasons why we left London to come to Minack.'

'The grit in the oyster.'

'And because of these pressures you haven't been able to put your mind to the flower farm as you used to do.'

'The old story of being unable to serve two masters.'

'Sooner or later we'll have to reconcile the two, and by going to London it might help. Afterwards we might see things in better perspective.'

'I doubt it,' I said, 'we'll have a gay time in London, a time of forgetting, that's all. When we get back we'll have to face facts. We'll have to make a choice. We'll have to decide whether to keep on the flower farm. And the only way to solve that problem is here at Minack.'

'You don't have to explain,' Jeannie said, and Lama was gently rubbing against her leg. 'I know you're right. We can't go on as we are. But in the meantime it would do you good to have a holiday.'

'You too. Especially now after the flower season.'

'Well?'

'I agree then,' I said, 'when do we go?'

Minack is a lonely spot with the nearest farm a half mile inland. The cottage sits snug by a wood, an old granite cottage with a massive chimney which in olden days was a beacon to sailing ships making their way across Mounts Bay to Newlyn. It has one large room, a small bedroom, and a spare room and bathroom. The site is carved out of a hillside and it faces, after a few hundred yards of moorland, the expanse of the bay. There is no other building except our old barn in sight, no road, no pylons, nothing to offend the view. The eyes peel across the gorse and the bracken, old hedges and boulders, to the sea and the distant shapes of houses far away on the Lizard peninsula.

Our fields slope down to the cliff, a hundred feet above the sea, then are replaced by a series of small meadows tumbling in odd shapes down to the rocks. Here grew our earliest daffodils, blooming so early in the year that they rivalled the pampered, heated daffodils that come from the vast glasshouses of Spalding. We had several tons of daffodils in our fourteen acres. We also had four large mobile greenhouses covering two sites, a small and a large static greenhouse in front of the cottage, and all of them were heated by oil burning heaters each with an electric fan. The fans drove the hot air through polythene ducting.

Had we foreseen, when we first came to Minack, such equipment and opportunity we would have been goggle eyed with excitement. We possessed then only our hands, enthusiasm and ignorance to drive us forward in the pursuit of making a living. We had no capital. There was no route for a car to reach the cottage. There was no water except the rain from the roof, and thus no bath. Our light came from paraffin lamps and candles and, as now, we had no telephone. But we had in our hearts the exquisitely sweet relief of being freed from twentieth-century entanglements. The deceptive gloss, the gritty worship of false values, the dependence on the decisions of tin gods, all these we had escaped from; and we had the years ahead of us in which to dwell with the primitive and to discover whether within ourselves we could earn contentment.

One discovers in these circumstances that one's own

shadow remains the enemy. During the honeymoon of the first years a magical impulse drives you forward, seducing you into believing that each set-back is a jest and each complication a momentary bad dream which has no reality in the life you are leading. It is easy to believe, at this time, that you have devised for yourself a way of life that for ever will be protected from the tendrils of computer civilization. You delude yourself into believing that you have the same freedom as an aborigine of the South American jungle. Cut off from the do-gooders and the progress makers you feel able to find your own level of happiness. Unharnessed by man-created shibboleths and conventions you feel you at last have the opportunity to release the forces of your secret self.

The balloon of these inspirations remains inflated until the setbacks and the complications begin monotonously to repeat themselves; and then it gradually dawns on you that the period of illusion is over, that it ended as abruptly as a school holiday without the merit of your knowing it, and that considerable determination will have to be exercised to stop yourself drifting.

Of course, it is pleasant to drift, as it is to lie in bed in the morning half awake. I was once a beachcomber on the island of Toopua two hundred miles south of Tahiti where my only neighbours were a Tahitian family; and I was contentedly able to develop a beachcomber mind because I knew my indulgence could not possibly last for long. I had a boat to catch and I had to come home.

There was, however, no timetable to govern our lives at Minack. Time was our own. We could lie in bed all morning if we wished, or treat hot summer days like holiday-makers, or start a job of work, get bored and give up. We had a roof over our heads in a setting we loved, and so long as we had enough to pay for our food we could wander along in indefinite idleness. A perpetual holiday, in fact, leading nowhere. The convential conception of the escapist.

We were able easily to reject such an attitude, but in doing so we made a miscalculation. We still imagined we could remain in isolation spiritually, if not materially, from the force of twentieth-century progress, and from the consortium of greed, envy and guile which sponsors the rat race.

Such a foolish error was due to the rawness of the life we led. Our pleasures were not designed for us at great expense by others. We had only to go and look out of the door, and whether the sun shimmered the Lizard in haze, or a raging storm thrust the foam and the waves into a darkening, winter sky, or the moon silvered the grey rocks that heaped around the cottage into the illusion of fairyland, we had only to see these things to shout to the heavens that we were alive. The sea breathed into our souls, the wind talked. We were part of the ageless striving of the human being. There around us, reflecting from the rough granite grey stones fingering up the walls of the cottage, were the calls of haymakers and the echo of carthorses, fishermen bringing their catch to the door, centuries of truthful endeavour, blazing summers, gales sweeping in from the south, justice in uncomplicated judgement, babies born and wagons carrying the old. All this we were aware of. All this elated every moment of our life at Minack. All this was our stronghold.

We had yet to learn that no one can escape from his shadow, and in order to survive in our new kind of life we had to compromise. We had to pay court to those who project the success of others. We had to flirt with the sponsors of the rat race. And by embracing the slippery, transient applause we faced losing what we had set out at Minack to achieve.

II

April is the between-time of a Cornish flower farm. Where once bloomed violets, anemones and daffodils, there are wastes of green. Soon the anemone plants are ploughed into the ground, and those of the violets split up into runners and planted again to flower the following winter. Only the daffodil beds remain and the foliage, as the summer advances, withers to yellow pointing to the moment when the bulbs, if need be, are dug, separated, sterilized and planted again.

It is a time of planning. Shall we have the violets again this year? They take much time to pick and to bunch. If the weather is kind they flower profusely and a glut is inevitable. If it is bad, prices may be high but there are few blooms. And anemones? They too are at the mercy of the weather, so could not the time involved in looking after them be better employed in other ways?

We had decided this April to streamline our programme. We would concentrate on crops in the greenhouses, except for the outdoor daffodils. Thus tomatoes were already planted in neat rows in the greenhouses, two thousand five hundred of them; and by the beginning of May we would have planted the freesia seeds. Some would go in a couple of thousand whalehide pots, and the rest would be planted in the open sites of two mobiles; and they would all be covered by glass as soon as the tomatoes were finished.

'Obviously,' I said firmly, 'this is the time to go for the holiday. Now. Immediately.'

'Hey!' said Jeannie, 'you take eight years to decide on going away, and now everything has to be arranged overnight.'

'I've got myself excited about it,' I said, 'I want to get away before any doubts set in.'

'Why should there be any doubts?'

'Doubts always set in if you stop to think.'

'Don't think then.'

'I'm not going to, but I have to plan. I have to plan the work for the student and arrange how he and his wife are going to look after Lama, Boris and the others.'

The student came from an agricultural college and was working for us while he looked for a place of his own to go to. He was the only help we had.

'What are you going to do about Lama, for instance?' I asked, 'she's never been left on her own before, and without us she might go wild again.'

'I think the best thing is to give her plenty of her favourite foods,' said Jeannie, 'and then we can hope that she will sleep most of the day.'

Lama came into our lives three years before. A mysterious arrival. The vet who then examined her said she was three months old, an exquisite little black kitten with one white whisker. It should have been easy to trace where she had come from because farms and cottages in our district are so few and far between. We visited each one for miles around. Nobody owned up to her. So where had she spent her first three months?

My first sight of her was at the beginning of that daffodil season, a black spot in the distance; but a couple of weeks later I was passing by a meadow of marigolds when I suddenly became aware of her scrutiny. She was three-quarters hidden within a mass of orange flowers, a small black velvet cushion with a pair of yellow eyes which followed me as I went by. I was acutely conscious of her steady stare; and I felt I was being assessed by a possible employer as to my qualifications in regard to a job.

My first touch of her was nearly disastrous. I found her one morning in the chicken run, and foolishly believing we could be friends I advanced to pick her up. Instead she hurtled herself against the wire netting, crazily tried to thrust her head through the small holes, then escaped from my fumbling hands by shooting up a tree and leaping like a monkey from one branch to another until she jumped clear, and disappeared into the wood.

Jeannie's approach was more subtle. She wooed her by placing saucers of milk at strategic places distant from the cottage, then reporting excitedly when the saucers were found to be empty. This courtship, this fencing between Lama and ourselves, continued until Easter Sunday afternoon when a tremendous storm blew in from the sea.

We were sitting in the cottage, the roar of the gale battering the walls and the roof, and Jeannie was reading her diary of almost exactly the year before. Monty, our old cat, was then dying and she read from her diary the account of the efforts she had made to save him. She also recalled what I had said to her at the time. I had said that as far as I was concerned, and she agreed, we would never have a cat again because we would never be able to repeat the love we had for Monty. Then I added, and this she also recalled, I would be ready to make one possible exception to this decision. That was if a cat, uninvited and untraceable, came crying to the door in a storm; but it had to be *black*.

Here we were then, on that Easter Sunday, sitting in the cottage when above the noise of the gale, I heard a miaow, and another, and another. I leapt from my chair, opened the cottage door; and into our lives came Lama.

Lama, therefore, while we were away, had to be suitably cared for, and so Jeannie decided she would have her favourites. Cod and whiting would be in the deep freeze, an emergency packet of Felix would be in the pantry; and to launch our departure there would be a special supply of pig's liver. Fed at steady intervals by the student and his wife, Lama would sleep and forget us. That, at any rate, was the aim.

There remained Boris, Knocker, Squeaker and Peter. Boris, the muscovy drake, had measured habits which had to be adhered to. He was a strong character who lived alone in the large one-time chicken house deep in the wood to which he retired without persuasion every evening as dusk was falling. He would waddle there, taking his time, then fly ponderously up on to his perch; and later we would come along to lock up his door and safeguard him from any prowling dangers of the night.

In the morning he could be difficult. He would explode in wrath if we were late in letting him out, hissing his fury and flapping his wings, charging after us as we returned to the cottage so that sometimes I have found myself murmuring: 'I'm sorry, Boris.'

He had arrived at Minack three years before in the arms of Jane, the young girl who then worked for us. A young farmer had attempted to woo her by bringing Boris in a sack to her cottage, and offering him for her dinner.

Her response was to burst out in anger, remove Boris quickly from the sack, and take him up to her bedroom where he remained for two days. Then her mother thought it was time for him to move, and Jane brought him to Minack.

His sense of independence, however, would make it easy to leave him. He enjoyed being undisturbed. He pottered about in the grass, dipped his yellow beak frequently in the pail of water kept full for the purpose, and two or three times a day plodded up the steep path to the door of the cottage for any titbits that might be available. He would, of course, miss these rewards, and Jeannie decided to compensate him by preparing a plentiful supply of his favourite home-made bread.

Knocker, Squeaker and Peter were the gulls. The first two were the owners of the roof, the latter a friendly, intelligent gull who arrived when the others were absent. Knocker and Squeaker fiercely defended their territory, and Peter would wait far off in a field until he saw the roof was clear; then sweep majestically towards us. I had a special fondness for Peter and he would sometimes go for walks with me. He would fly and swoop over my head, alight on a boulder a few yards ahead of me, then surge into the sky again when I reached him. Knocker and Squeaker were more opportunist. They would parade the apex of the roof day after day, and in the winter would squat side by side on the chimney, content with its warmth. When they were hungry, if we had failed to attend to their needs, Squeaker would squeak and Knocker would bang on the roof with his beak. Many a time he has deceived us into thinking there was someone at the door, so insistent, so loud has been his knock. These three also had to be looked after. They were not, however, going to be pampered. They did not like shop bread but they would have to put up with it.

All the instructions for the student and his wife were neatly typed. We had bought our tickets to Paddington. We had decided to stay at the Savoy, the first time together there since Jeannie had written 'MEET ME AT THE SAVOY'. We both had a pleasant sense of anticipation of the gay time ahead. It was Friday and we were going to leave by the Sunday night train. Everything, in fact, about the holiday was organized, when the Lamorna postmaster strode down the lane with a telegram. The message said simply:

> 'Got donkey.
>   Teague.'

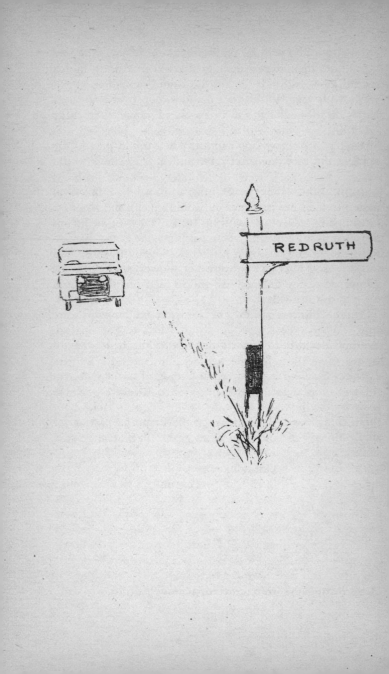

III

I looked at the telegram in dismay.

'Heavens, Jeannie,' I said, 'now what do we do?'

Mr Teague, a Dickensian, toby jug of a man, kept the Plume of Feathers at Scorrier near Redruth. He was also a cattle dealer, a horse dealer, a dealer in any kind of animal. We had had a drink with him a couple of weeks previously.

'I never said *definitely* I wanted one,' she murmured. 'I only *talked* to him about it. I never thought he had taken me seriously.'

I glanced at her suspiciously.

'You promise you didn't make some secret plan with him? . . . arrange for him to produce a donkey just as you arranged with your mother to give us Monty? . . . presenting me with a *fait accompli*?'

'Don't be silly.'

'You've always been so dotty about donkeys that I could believe anything.'

Her addiction to donkeys began when she first learnt to toddle. Her family were living in Scotland, and they used to take their holidays at Troon; here on the sands Jeannie was given her first donkey ride. Her mother looked back on the event as a mixed blessing; for the ride was such a success that every morning when Jeannie woke up her first words were: 'I want a donkey ride.' She would have first one ride, then another, and when her mother, aiming at discipline, refused to allow a third, Jeannie would howl. Her mother in a desperate need to silence her would offer a compromise, a visit after the morning play on the sands to where the donkeys were tethered. Jeannie used to arrive at the spot, look up at them high above her, then put out a tiny hand to stroke their soft noses.

Her next encounter with donkeys was when her family began taking their holidays in the Isles of Scilly. The islands in those days had the remoteness associated with islands. There was no mass invasion of holiday makers. There were no telephone kiosks or cars, and electricity was limited to those who made their own. It was a magical place to visit, sailing, fishing, lying in the sun on deserted beaches, somewhere in which time seemed to be poised in space. The war was close, but Jeannie and her friends used to play there, deaf to the noise of the dictators, gloriously believing there was no end to any day, bronzed youth swimming in still blue water, shouting to the heavens their relish of living.

She used to stay in those days in the Atlantic Hotel on St Mary's overlooking the harbour. And when she was there in the spring she used to lean out of her bedroom window in the early morning and watch entranced the sight of the donkeys and their little green carts bringing the daffodil boxes to the quay. Then she dressed and went down to the breakfast tables and took lumps of sugar from the bowls. Many a donkey was pleased to see her as it waited for its cart to be unloaded.

And later in the day she used to make a regular sortie to a field where a favourite donkey was put out to graze. First there was one donkey, then another and another. She had the childish delight in fancying that the donkeys had gossiped as they stood by the quay, spreading the news that a girl visited a certain field with a pocketful of sugar. Then one day there were more than twenty donkeys in the field, and it was not fun any more. They barged their noses into her pockets, pushed and shoved her, until she became frightened and began to run away from them. Her father who was watching her said it was a very funny sight ... the Florence Nightingale of the donkeys racing across the grass and twenty sugar-mad donkeys close behind her.

I also had been chased by a donkey.

My earliest memory, so distant that I sometimes wonder whether it may be my imagination at work, is lying in a steep grass field staring up at the grey underbelly of a donkey. The field itself, and this I remember clearly, fell from the road to the seashore at the river end of Porth beach near my childhood home at Newquay. I was very small, and in my haste and terror as I ran from the donkey I had tripped, tumbling over into the grass, desperately aware that my future lay at the mercy of the beast which was soon upon me.

I am able to believe in the reality of my story so far, but there is also an event in my memory so horrifying that it is strange that no one in my family can vouch for it. My mother when she was alive, and when I asked her about it, laughed at my foolishness, and surely she would have remembered so violent an incident to her youngest son.

The donkey, so my memory tells me, kicked me in the teeth as I lay helpless beneath him.

This memory, or childish nightmare as it must have been, was vividly present during my conversation with Jeannie. Donkeys, as cats had once been, were to me unfriendly creatures; but whereas my original distaste for cats was merely because I thought them vulgar, detached and selfish, I was, as far as donkeys were concerned, a little scared.

They were bony and heavy, and dull witted. I did not see how one could trust a donkey. A cat at least was not dangerous. It might scratch when frightened, or might even lacerate you if enraged, and you happened to be in the way. That was all. A donkey, on the other hand, was an unruly creature. It might kick without reason. Or bite. It was uncouth. I could not foresee how a donkey could ever enter the stream of our life except to excite our pity. There it would stand forlornly in a meadow, nothing to do, reproachfully demanding our attention which it would be too stupid to appreciate.

Jeannie, of course, had long ago forgiven her sugar-mad donkeys, and I guessed she only needed a little encouragement from me for her to answer the telegram by setting out forthwith to have a look at the donkey. I, on the other hand, remained on guard.

'The first thing I'm going to do,' I told her, 'is to have a word with Jack Baker.'

Jack Baker was a landscape gardener, and at this time was designing a new part of our garden. He was a practical man, an expert horticulturalist, a mechanic, a tree feller and, what interested me particularly, he had had experience with donkeys.

'Tell me, Jack,' I said when I found him, 'what do you think about keeping a donkey as a pet?'

Jack had a merry eye but a lugubrious nature. He wanted to enjoy life but the fates had checked him so many times that he was inclined always to outline the tedious side of a problem at the expense of the happier side. He was in his fifties, tall and broad-shouldered, an individualist who, during the war, preferred to remain a sergeant in the Guards rather than accept the commission he was offered. He was one of those rare people one would instinctively want to be with in a jam. He would, I felt sure, be calm while the threat – whatever it was – received his attention. I anxiously awaited his donkey views.

He took the pipe from his mouth, knocked the ash from the bowl on a rock, then pronounced:

'You'll have a packet of trouble.'

I was, of course, prepared for a douche of cold water. He was only being true to my knowledge of him, a harbinger of bad news before good; and yet his attitude, because it coincided with my own, was pleasing to listen to.

'How do you mean?' I asked.

'Well, the first thing you'll find out, for instance,' he said solemnly, 'is that it will eat up the garden.'

Even to my ears this remark sounded biased. What about a horse or a cow? Wouldn't they eat up the garden if they were given a chance?

Jack was leaning on his shovel, amused, delighting in his mission to discomfort me.

'Ah,' he said knowingly. 'A horse or a cow can be kept in a field, and it's only bad luck if it gets out. But a donkey! You can't keep a donkey loose in a field. It'll get out. It'll jump a fence or a wall, and go roaming all over the district. And it'll be eating up other people's gardens besides yours.'

'What do people do about donkeys then?'

He grinned at me.

'Best thing to do is to tether it. You get a swivel anchor from the blacksmith, fix it firmly in the ground, and the donkey goes round and round eating the grass. Then twice a day you move it.'

'Twice a day?'

'Oh yes, otherwise as soon as it has eaten the grass it will start braying.'

'It's a bit of a job digging up the anchor and then fixing it again, isn't it?'

'Certainly. But that's what people do.'

I could not see myself doing it.

'There's another point,' Jack went on, and he was now talking as if he believed he had got me on the run, 'and that's water. A donkey drinks a lot, and you'll have to keep a bucket always full beside it. If a donkey is thirsty even for a minute the braying will start up.'

'How loud is the braying?'

'They'll hear it in the next parish.'

'But surely,' I said, 'you're exaggerating. You're making out that a donkey is only fit for a zoo. After all, lots of people *do* keep donkeys.'

'Not for long. They're excited when they get them at

23

first but soon tire of them when they find out the trouble they cause.'

I found at this moment, contrary to reason, that Jack's attitude was engaging my sympathy for donkeys. His arguments against them seemed, even to me, to be overloaded.

'Now tell me honestly,' I said, 'how *friendly* can a donkey be?'

He sat down on a rock, put his palms on his knees, laughingly looked at me with his head on one side, and replied:

'How friendly? You ask me how friendly? . . . all I can say I would never dare keep a donkey myself!'

This should have been enough to make up my mind. Armed with Jack's arguments I could have gone to Jeannie and explained to her that a donkey at Minack was quite impracticable. He had confirmed my suspicions. A donkey would only be a nuisance.

But there were other factors involved which I felt would be fair to consider. Jack himself, for instance. He knew us both well enough to realize that in any case Jeannie would have her donkey if she really wished, and, therefore, he could without qualms take humorous pleasure in trying to scare me. He had had his joke but, contrarily, he had awakened my interest. My talk with him had the effect of an appetizer; and I was beginning to be intrigued as to where the ownership of a donkey might lead me.

I had also to admit that Minack would provide a wonderful setting for a donkey. It could roam along the grey boulders of the moorland, wander down the steep slopes of the cliff to the sea's edge, and for most of the year when the daffodils were not growing, it could be loose in the bulb fields. There was land enough, therefore, for it not to have any reason to escape; and I also saw a practical advantage. A donkey would help to keep the grass down.

Nor could I forget that in the past I had always objected to the arrival of a new pet, and then soon agreed that my objections had been wrong. I had not wanted Monty or Lama or the drake or the fox cub which Jeannie looked after when it was brought to her with an injured foot. I suffered the contradictory emotions of enjoying responsibility once it had been imposed upon me, but of fearing any addition to those I already held. An animal was a responsibility. I had been brought up to believe that once an animal is accepted into a household it must be treated as a member of it, and not as a piece of furniture. And I remember my father telling me, when he gave me my first puppy, that it was my job to make the puppy happy, and not the other way round.

I was, therefore, in two minds what to do; and in the end I decided to surprise Jeannie. I would act in a holiday spirit. When she set out to persuade me to go and have a look at the donkey, I would immediately agree. What harm could there be in just having a look?

So an hour later we were in the Land-Rover, and I was innocently driving towards Mr Teague. We were about to arrive when Jeannie suddenly said, 'If we like it, we will have the donkey, won't we?'

'No,' I said firmly, 'certainly not.'

And I knew I was lying.

IV

We reached the Plume of Feathers soon after opening time, and Mr Teague greeted us with a glint in his eye. He saw a sale in the offing.

'Come in,' he said jovially from behind the bar, 'have a drink. What'll you have, Mrs Tangye?'

Mr Teague, or Roy as he now insisted on us calling him, was in the fortunate position of being able to do his bargaining on his own licensed premises. Sales could be conducted in convivial circumstances, and though a purchaser might succeed in reducing a price or a seller in increasing it, the cost of the evening had to be considered. I was aware of this. I had therefore decided, in the event of us wishing to buy the donkey, to complete the deal with the minimum of argument. I might lose a pound or two on the price, but this was a sensible sacrifice if it meant we could speedily return to Minack.

'We've just looked in to see the donkey,' I said casually, 'it was very nice of you to send the telegram.'

'Not at all,' he said, 'I've got a nice little donkey and thought I'd let you have the first chance.'

He had got us our drinks and was now leaning with elbows on the bar, hands interlocked. I could see he was about to turn his charm on Jeannie. She was a vulnerable target.

'Lovely tempered little donkey,' he said, smiling at her, 'good as gold. Comes from Ireland, from Connemara or somewhere like that. They ship them over by the dozen these days.'

'What for?'

'They go for pet food mostly.'

27

'How cruel,' said Jeannie.

He was now fiddling with an empty ash tray on the counter.

'The only trouble is she is not in very good condition. Nothing serious. Nothing that Dr Green can't soon put right.'

'Dr Green?' I asked, puzzled.

'Grass.'

'Oh, of course.'

He turned again to Jeannie. His eyes were twinkling.

'And there's another thing. Something, I bet, you never bargained for when you came along here. She's in foal. Two donkeys for one. What about that?'

I took a gulp at my drink.

'Good heavens!' I said.

'Now, now, now,' he answered, looking at me and sensing a momentary set-back, 'as soon as she's had the foal I'll buy it off you. Nothing could be fairer than that, could it?'

He turned again to Jeannie.

'Have you ever seen a little donkey foal? Lovely little things they are. Just like a toy. You can pick it up in your arms. I've seen a child do that, honestly I have.'

I watched Jeannie melting. The practical side, the prospect of *two* donkeys charging about Minack did not concern her at all. All that she could imagine was the picture card idyll of a donkey and its foal. The deal was advancing in his favour. Somewhere in a field behind the pub was a donkey which was on the brink of being ours.

And then Mr Teague played his ace.

'Sad thing about this donkey,' he said, fumbling again with the ash tray, 'very sad thing . . . by the way, Penny's her name. Pretty name Penny, isn't it?'

'You were saying.'

'Yes, I was going to tell you that if you don't like the look of her, I've got a buyer. Made a good offer he has too, but it's a sad story.'

28

'Why so sad?'

'Well, I wouldn't like to see it happen. You see the idea of this buyer is to wait for the foal to be born, then put it in a circus. A donkey foal in a circus would be a big draw, especially on the holiday circuit. Can't you see the children flocking round it?'

I could see he was genuinely concerned.

'What happens to the mother?'

He glanced at me, appreciating that I was on the wavelength.

'That's the point. That's what I'm worried about. That's why I want to find her a good home, and thought of you two.'

'How do you mean?'

'The idea of this buyer friend of mine is to send Penny to the knacker's yard as soon as the youngster can get along without her.'

'But that's awful.' I could not help myself from saying what I knew was in Jeannie's mind.

'And what's more,' went on Roy Teague, 'when the season is over and they've got their money's worth out of the youngster, it'll be too big to keep.' He paused. 'They'll send it to the knacker's yard as well.'

The emotion he expected erupted.

'I must go and see her at once.' Jeannie was picking up the gloves she had dropped on a stool. She looked pained. She was at that moment the ideal example of a salesman's victim. She was hooked, and so was I. However bad was the donkey's condition, we must buy her. It was our duty. We had been given the chance of saving her, and of giving a home for her foal. Here was an opportunity which reached far beyond our original inclinations. We would not only be giving a donkey a home, but also acquiring a donkey which would otherwise be doomed ... first by sadness because of being parted too soon from her foal, then by the journey which ended in the knacker's yard. I was a donkey buyer with a mission. I had better begin negotiations.

'You go ahead,' I said to Jeannie, 'have a look at her and see what you think. I'll have another drink.'

My purpose in not accompanying her was to appear nonchalant in front of Mr Teague. I intended to go through the form of bargaining, the pause between sentences, the changes of subject, the sudden return to a point that appeared to be forgotten, the mock laughter over a price which in reality I didn't think too high, the pretence that I had, in fact, no intention of wanting the donkey at all; all those machinations which one feels one ought to pursue despite the fact that an immediate deal would produce a shout of joy.

'I suppose you're getting ready for the season,' I said, after Jeannie had disappeared to the paddock behind the pub where the donkey was temporarily grazing, 'all ready for the rush.'

'That's right. Winter in a hammock, then a sprint.'

'I don't know how you stand it night after night.'

'It's a job. Like any job you have to stick to it.'

'Not for me. I wouldn't stand it for any money.'

He took my glass, and swung round to the optics.

'Mrs Tangye is dead keen on that donkey, isn't she?' He had his back to me, a finger on the lever of the optic of the whisky bottle. 'Dead keen, I should say.'

He was forcing the pace.

'She's always liked donkeys ever since she was a child,' I said, as if I were talking about the weather, 'of course she's got a kind heart, and that story you told her upset her a bit.'

'It's true.'

'Now, Roy,' I felt that I could sound intimate, 'I believe you are a fair man. What price have you in mind for the donkey?'

He looked at me shrewdly, bright eyes from a red, jovial

face. He had no intention of exploiting me, that I was sure; but naturally he would like to make a maximum profit. He pushed my glass across the counter.

'Have it for twenty-seven pounds.'

I fumbled for a packet of cigarettes, found it, pulled out one, lit it. I apparently succeeded by this delay in conveying to him that the figure had shocked me.

'I'll tell you what I'll do,' he said, speaking quickly, 'I'll throw in a shay with the price. A donkey and a shay go together, everyone used them in the old days. It's good fun. If the car breaks down I can see Penny taking you and Mrs Tangye into Penzance!'

I couldn't, but I joined in his laughter.

'It's worth five pound,' he said.

At this moment, before I could answer, the door at the corner of the lounge was flung open, and in rushed Jeannie. One glance at her and I knew the donkey was ours, whatever the price, whatever its condition. Roy looked at her happily.

'She came to me as soon as I called her!' she said excitedly, 'came right across the field as if she knew me, as if...'

'I know, I know,' I said, 'as if she knew you were the one person in the world who could give her a happy home.'

She ignored me.

'... as if she were hungry.'

'Not much grass in that paddock, true enough,' said Roy, 'but you'll soon put her to rights. Eat anything, donkeys will.'

'Now look,' I said, trying to sound sensible, 'there are one or two things we ought to clear up. How old is she, for instance?'

'She's four. Can't be more than four.'

'And what about the foal. When is the foal expected?'

'A month perhaps. Five weeks. Difficult to say.'

Then he added quickly.

'I'll buy the foal back, mind. Give you ten quid, I promise.'

A promise I knew would never be put to the test.

'And what,' I went on, 'does one do about the confinement?'

'Leave her out,' he said briskly, 'leave her out and she'll look after herself. No trouble at all.'

I envied his casual efficiency. All his life he had been accustomed to the arrival and the departure of animals; and he was naturally impatient with my doubts as to how to treat properly a donkey and its foal. They were a production unit as far as he was concerned. Something which could make a sale and a profit and, without being heartless, something he considered as inanimate as tins in a grocery shop. He would never carry on his business as a dealer had he thought otherwise. And yet I felt he was sentimental enough to be glad that Penny was about to leave for a good home.

'Well,' I said, 'about the price. We don't want the shay, you can keep that. I'll give you a cheque for twenty-five pounds.'

'That'll do me.'

'What about the delivery charge. Who's going to pay that? I mean we'll have to hire a horse box.'

He grinned at me, giving the empty ash tray another twirl with his finger.

'Don't need a horse box. Got a Land-Rover outside haven't you? Put her in that. My daughter fetched a donkey in one from Exeter the other day. No trouble at all.'

This was a situation I had not foreseen. Indeed had I had an inkling when I set out for the Plume of Feathers that I would leave it with a donkey in the back, I would have stayed at home.

'But surely she might be dangerous,' I remonstrated

32

weakly, conscious I risked being labelled a coward, 'she might get in a panic as I was driving along, lash out and all that. She might bite.'

I hoped that Jeannie would agree.

'Come and see her,' she said soothingly, as if I were making a fool of myself, 'she's as quiet as an old sheep dog. I certainly don't mind myself if she comes with us.'

And she did.

Half an hour later we were racing along the Redruth by-pass with me at the wheel, Jeannie beside me, and between the two of us, shoulder level, the solemn, patient face of Penny the donkey.

V

'You know, Jeannie,' I said, as we turned off the by-pass and drove up the hill into Camborne, 'we've got ourselves in a fix. We can't possibly leave a donkey which is going to have a foal.'

'I realize that too.'

'So that's the end of our holiday before it's begun.'

'Are you very disappointed?'

'It seems to me to be sheer lunacy to give up a long overdue holiday just because we take pity on a wretched donkey.'

We were passing the Holman engineering works on our left, and the road to Illogan where my grandfather was born on our right.

'Turn round and take her back then.'

'I'm thinking,' I went on ignoring Jeannie, 'of all the trouble involved in putting everything off. What do I say? And how is your mother going to react when you tell her you can't go to London because we've bought a donkey in the family way?'

'She'll laugh.'

A huge lorry ahead slowed us down to a crawl.

'I had got myself attuned to the idea of seeing the bright lights again. I was looking forward to a frivolous time.'

'You can go on your own.'

'Don't be silly.'

'There's such a change in you. First I have to knock you on the head to make you go, and now you're moaning away because you can't.'

'My contrary self.'

I changed gear, accelerated and passed the lorry blow-ing the horn. I found comfort in doing so.

'It means,' I said, 'we won't have the chance of going away again for a year. You know that. We won't have a chance what with the tomatoes, the freesias, the daffodils all following on each other. We're committed to fight it out this year.'

'You can write a book about the year in between.'

'Between what?'

'The year in which you decide whether to work with your mind or work with your hands. The year in which we decide whether to continue with the flower farm.'

'It is a question of labour. There is so much manual work to be done. That's all the trouble.'

'Cheer up. You're forgetting you're going to have another interest.'

'What?'

'A year with two donkeys!'

At this moment Penny, who was standing in the well of the Land-Rover and small enough to be clear of the canvas hood, pushed her head forward and, to my concern, rested it on my shoulder. Thus, as I stared at the road ahead of me lined at first by squat houses and shops, then by the open fields leading to Connor Downs and Hayle, I could see out of the corner of my eye a large white nose; and I felt a weight on my shoulder like the hand of someone wanting to reassure me.

'She seems to like you.'

'I think I'm dotty.'

'But don't you feel happier?'

'I suppose so.'

'You're a misery!'

The time was seven o'clock and we had a little over an hour before dusk. Clouds were looming up over the distant Zennor hills, hiding the sun. Penny's head remained resting on my shoulder, and I took one hand off the wheel and stroked her nose. Even so early in her life with us, she was placid. It was if she had had many journeys such as this one, shifted from one place to another, railway trucks, the boat from Ireland, cattle lorries, herded with other donkeys at auction sales; and these experiences had made her resigned. Here she was travelling to another paddock, another brief period of affection or work, then on to somewhere else as soon as the originality of her presence had worn thin, or her usefulness had expired.

We were nearing Connor Downs.

'Let's stop for a drink at the Turnpike,' I said. I said it doubtfully. I was prepared for Jeannie to say that one didn't leave a donkey in charge of a car while one went inside a pub.

'All right, but I'll stay with her. We have to get her out of the Land-Rover before it is dark. We can't be long.'

I had good reason to stop at the Turnpike. Jack Edwards, the landlord, had been a gamekeeper for most of his life, and whenever Jeannie and I wanted experienced advice on a section of country life he could be relied upon to supply it. A few weeks before, for instance, we had called in to see him about a dying fox we had found in the lane a few hundred yards from the cottage.

Foxes and badgers are numerous around Minack, and often in the early morning we can lie in bed watching a fox through the window nosing about the field opposite. We pretend to ourselves, and we may be right, that we can identify each one. This particular spring there had been two dog foxes we had watched, one whose territory seemed to be the field opposite, the other who spent his time in a neighbouring one. I would watch them through field-glasses stalking a mouse in the grass, alert and ears cocked, a pause before the pounce, then the attack and the spread-eagling of legs like a cat. We were amused when the attempt misfired. There was the same posture of disappointment, then the same nonchalant pretence that failure did not matter which we had seen so often displayed by

Monty and Lama.

One of these two, the one in the neighbouring field, appeared to be younger than the other. He seemed to be bigger, a better sheen on his coat, and his brush was huge. He was also more adventurous and we would often watch him slink over the hedge before darkness fell, then up and over and along the track that led away from the cliff country into the hinterland. And then in the morning we would watch him return, tongue hanging out, a tired fox, and we would wonder how many miles he had travelled; and of the angry conversation someone at that very moment might be having about a fox that had raided the poultry during the night.

One evening soon after dusk we were still bunching daffodils in the packing shed when we heard a scream up the lane as wild as that of a hyena. Then another and another, such a cacophony that it was as if there had been a collision of screams. After ten minutes, during which time there were momentary silences and a gradual lessening of the noise as it moved away up the lane, I said to Jeannie that we had better go and find out what had happened. We did not really expect to find anything. We were just being curious.

We had gone half-way towards the farm at the top without seeing anything and were about to turn back when my torch shone on what looked like a dog curled up in the middle of the lane. As we walked closer it began to move, dragging its body towards the ditch; and we saw it was a fox. There was nothing we could do except to leave it without it being frightened by the sight of us. We saw that its front paws were terribly mangled and it could not possibly go far whatever its other injuries. We left it lying in the ditch and half an hour later when I returned it was dead.

The following morning through our bedroom window we saw the field opposite was empty, but the neighbouring one had its usual occupant, the splendid-looking young dog fox. As we watched, he jumped over the hedge into the field which hitherto had been forbidden to him, and began wandering around as if he owned it. The same thing happened morning after morning, and so we concluded that he had fought and killed his rival, and he was the new king of the territory.

In due course I had described the episode to Jack Edwards. I also told him that a trapper I knew had said that our conclusion was wrong. The trapper maintained that a young badger had been the killer. Who was right?

'When the fighting was going on,' asked Jack Edwards, 'did you hear any grunting noises?'

'None at all.'

'Badgers grunt when they fight.'

'There was only an endless screaming.'

'That confirms your conclusion was correct and the trapper was wrong.'

'What happened then?'

'Foxes fight on their hind legs like horses. They box each other. I reckon the young fox was quick enough to seize the old one's paws as they fought, and that's why they were mangled. That's what happened.'

I now turned the Land-Rover off the main road and drew up in the Turnpike car-park.

There was no one else in the bar.

'Jack,' I said, coming straight to the point which was still bothering me, 'are donkeys difficult to keep?'

'How do you mean?'

'Are they the asses they're supposed to be?'

He lit a cigarette and smiled.

'I've known some intelligent donkeys in the past. Like everyone else some are clever, some are not.'

'Can they be a nuisance?'

'They're certainly very affectionate.'

'Which means?'

'They need a lot of attention . . . but what's all this about?'

At this moment there was a wail outside like that of a banshee. A gargling noise on a high note.

'Heavens,' I said, 'she's calling me!'

'Who?'

'The donkey.'

'God bless my soul!'

'We've just bought one from Roy Teague.'

'What about Mrs Tangye . . . where's she?'

'She's out there too.'

'Mrs Tangye guarding the donkey? . . . Look, I'm taking her a drink straight away.'

We went outside and up to the Land-Rover; and as Jack walked forward, glass in hand, a face was thrust through the driver's window. It had a large white nose.

'I sign the pledge!' cried Jack.

Penny pushed her head forward as if she were making to bite the glass. She looked quite fierce. I did not realize until later that she was only thirsty.

But at the same time an unpleasant thought crossed my mind. She was showing restlessness. She might, for all I knew, be vicious. Dusk would be falling when we reached Minack, and Penny in a strange place without an expert to handle her might not be so placid at her journey's end as she had been at the beginning.

How were we to remove her from the Land-Rover on our own?

VI

Rain began to spatter the windscreen as we turned from the main road into the bumpy lane which led a mile away to Minack. Clouds, low and lugubrious, swirling in from the sea and the south, were hastening the dusk to fall before its time.

'I feel very pleased with myself,' said Jeannie suddenly.

'Why's that?'

'Well,' she said, 'before we left and when you were out of sight, I got hold of Jack Baker and asked him a favour.'

'And what was this favour?'

'It was his idea really.'

'Come on, tell me what it was.'

I felt irked that I had not been previously informed.

'You know that big iron bar which is used for levering rocks?'

'Of course I do.'

'Jack Baker suggested it would make an ideal tethering post for a donkey.'

'Reasonable enough.'

'And so before we set off just in case we *did* buy a donkey, I asked him to fix it.'

'You seemed very certain in that case that we *would* buy a donkey.'

'The only trouble is,' she said, ignoring me, 'that he couldn't put it upright as the soil was too shallow. He therefore planned to anchor it into the ground horizontally, helped by a couple of big rocks at either end of the bar.'

A journey into detail was unlike her. She was hiding something.

'The bar,' she went on, 'is all in the ground except

where the rope is tied. The other end of the rope we join to the halter we've brought with us. It means that Penny can't run away.'

We passed the jumble of farm buildings which stood at the top of the valley, then began to descend the last stretch to the cottage. And all the time Penny's head rested firmly on my shoulder.

'Whereabouts,' I asked, 'am I going to find this contraption?'

'On the lawn.'

I calmed myself. I kept my hands on the wheel. I said nothing.

'I know what you're thinking,' she went on, 'I can guess. But . . . honestly, it isn't much of a lawn. Now is it?'

'I should certainly think not after you and Jack Baker and the donkey have carved it up.'

'Don't be silly.'

'What do you expect me to say? You've seen me enough times cursing and sweating, keeping the grass cut with the motor scythe, the most exhausting machine ever devised.'

'It still isn't really a lawn.'

'It was improving.'

'Where else can we put her? The stable is full up with junk and we couldn't possibly clear it out tonight. And if we put her in a field she might jump over the hedge and be lost.'

'I suppose it never occurred to you that you could have put the contraption in a field?'

'Oh yes,' said Jeannie softly, 'I thought of that, but you see, she would be lonely. By having her on the lawn I can keep a watch on her through the bedroom window.'

'All night?'

'Every now and then I could look out and see she's all right.'

'Are you sure you wouldn't like me to carry out an armchair? You could sit beside her under an umbrella.'

'What a good idea!' she said laughing.

There was a jerk as the Land-Rover went through the stream that crosses the entrance to Minack, the stream we call Monty's Leap. It was here, when at last we had arrived at Minack, that on a magical moonlight night Monty had nosed his way puzzlingly down the lane; and on reaching the stream had ignored my readiness to lift him over and, instead, had leapt majestically across. It was here, too, beside this stream that he was buried.

'Hell,' I said, 'it's started to pour.'

I drew up outside the cottage and as I did so I saw the rain dancing on the bonnet; and when I switched off the engine I could hear the wind sweeping through the elm trees.

'It's going to be a dirty old night.'

'What a beginning for her.'

'She's got to get used to it sometime. And, anyhow, didn't she come from Ireland?'

'That doesn't mean she *enjoys* rough weather.'

'Nor do we. And we are about to be soaked trying to lure a donkey from the back of a Land-Rover towards a contraption outside our bedroom window, and keeping it from running away.'

'I'm ready.'

The lawn has a steep slope, the size of half a tennis court, and a section of the bottom end merged with the parking space for cars. I proceeded to back the Land-Rover to this spot so that when the rear was unlatched the well of the Land-Rover was level, within a yard or two, of the lawn. Hence Penny had only to jump this short distance to be on firm ground. Unfortunately her bottom faced the wrong way.

'Come on, Penny,' I said, gently pulling the rope of the halter, 'turn round.'

She stayed staring across the front seats at the windscreen.

'Do *please* turn round.'

I pulled again, firmly this time. It was like pulling a tree trunk.

'For heaven's sake, Penny, TURN ROUND.'

No response.

'I'll get a carrot,' said Jeannie, running indoors and returning with a handful.

'Look Penny,' I said, tugging at her again and holding a carrot like a flag, 'look what I've got.'

There was an imperceptible movement of her head, an intimation that she was giving me a sideways glance, no immediate surrender to greed but one sensed a thought was passing through her mind; when did I last have one of these delectable things?

I pushed the carrot up to her face, then cunningly traced it along the side of the canvas hood so that she had to turn her head to watch it. I knew victory was near. The ancient carrot trick was about to work. I stood at the open end of the Land-Rover and waited.

She did a neat turn. The well of the Land-Rover is only four feet by three, a small space for a donkey in foal, but she manoeuvred herself with the ease of a large dog. Her bottom to the driving seat, her face thrust forward, peering into the rain and growing darkness, she now expected her reward.

'I'll let her have a nibble,' I said, 'just to whet her appetite. Then I'll do the trick again to get her out.'

Her idea of a nibble was to grab the carrot from my hand. A huge mouth, then crunch, crunch, crunch. It was a succulent sound, the forerunner of many, many such crunches. Here was enjoyment of high degree, the luscious favourite dish of a gourmet, the wild abandon of someone who had forgotten good manners in the pursuit of exquisite flavours. I felt, as I listened, my own mouth watering, and I thought of my supper, and I cursed the rain. Penny might be enjoying herself but it was time we reached the comfort of the cottage.

'Here you are,' I said, dangling another carrot invitingly, as I stood on the lawn three yards from the crunch. 'Here you are,' I said again.

I have learnt now that you do not eat a carrot in the way you eat a handful of hay or a slice of bread. These are ordinary things. A carrot requires respect, and after the crunch there follows the lick. The purpose of the lick is to recapture the original delight, an attempt to linger the pleasure, mirrored by an indulgent look in the eyes of the licker. The licker prefers to lick a hand, or a stone if it is handy, but it can be perfectly satisfied by its own solid looking mouth. In any case, the observer, the provider of the carrot, must be patient.

'Look, look,' I said, backing away up the slope, 'another carrot!'

I felt the rain filtering between my neck and the collar of my shirt, while Jeannie, scarf over her head, was clutching the rest of the carrots, allowing me to conduct the campaign on my own. Both of us were growing impatient.

Lick, lick; like a cat after a capture.

'Come on, Penny,' I said, 'jump out into your new home.'

She did not jump, she scrambled; and in one awful moment three of her legs were on the ground while the other was left sprawling in the Land-Rover.

'Look out, she'll break her leg,' cried Jeannie.

'I'm doing my best!'

I was holding the halter, unsure whether to let it lie loose so that she could make her own recovery, or to pull it tight and so attempt to pull her with it. And I was angry with myself. I was angry that we should have been so foolish as to bring her home in such conditions of rain and darkness and ignorance. We should have gone back for her in the morning, or at any rate stopped at the farm at the top and asked Jack Cochram, the farmer, to come down and help us. It had been laziness on my part, or a vain wish to prove my independence, and Penny was paying for it.

But, as it happened, in this instant of my panic I had over-dramatized the situation. My habit of seeing disaster before it has occurred danced me to a conclusion which was quite invalid. Penny, realizing her predicament, paused a few seconds to gain balance on the three legs already on the ground, then leapt forward bringing the fourth one clear.

'Our first lesson,' I said, mockingly serious, 'let her look after herself.'

For Jeannie, however, this was not a lesson that was easy to accept as I learnt during the course of the night. A donkey in the darkness of a strange place, standing in driving rain and a gale, was certain to excite her pity.

We tied Penny to the contraption on the lawn, fed her with a pound of carrots, three apples and half a loaf of home-made bread, and put a pail of water beside her. The adventure, as far as I was concerned, was over for the time being. I wanted my own supper, and a good night's sleep.

But Jeannie had no such intention. Twice during supper she dashed outside with a torch; and when we went to bed, no sooner had I turned out the light than she was at the window gleaming the torch through the rain at the bedraggled donkey ten yards away on the lawn.

'Poor thing,' she murmured.

'Hell to it,' I replied, 'I want to go to sleep.'

I awoke soon after dawn and I lay there listening to the dawn chorus, sleepily attempting to identify the many songs. The storm had passed and it was still again; and through the window I could see the crescent of the sun climbing behind the Lizard. It was a heavenly morning, and for a brief moment I believed I possessed no cares. Then suddenly I realized why I had woken so early.

There, just outside the bedroom window, was a donkey.

A responsibility. I had waited for years for a holiday and I had sacrificed it to a four-legged creature which would be useless for any practical purpose. There would be nothing for it to do except mooch about demanding attention. And soon there would be the foal. Two donkeys mooching about.

They would live for years and years; and every day I would be waking up, half worrying what to do with them. Should they be in this meadow or that? Have they got enough water? We had burdened ourselves with two large permanent pets, remote in manner but utterly dependent upon us. I had been rushed into making a purchase that any cool period of thinking would have made me check, see reason, and halt from making. On this lovely, fresh early morning I was angry with myself.

And then I found myself wondering why I was vexed. True I had made an unreasonable, over-excited gesture, but it was a gesture which tied me even more closely to Minack; and Minack was a home neither of us would ever want to leave. So why was there a demon inside me who resented another anchor?

I lay thinking and was unable to answer. There was just this vague, tenuous sense of distress that I had committed myself. Perhaps I had discovered for myself the reason why so many are scared of the affection of animals. They do not want to be tied. They do not want anchors. Their lives are complicated enough without having to worry about a creature on four legs.

I was fully awake by now. I also found that a curiosity was already replacing my negative thoughts. How was she? What was she doing?

I got out of bed and looked out of the window.

Penny was happily eating the lawn I hadn't cut for a month.

VII

Penny was black, and this had disappointed me from the first moment I saw her. Only the bottom half of her nose, the rims round her eyes, and a rotund girth were white or a light grey. I felt as I did when, years ago, I went to Tahiti and found the sands which edged the lagoons were black. In both cases my preconceived ideas had been affronted; sands of the South Seas should be white, coat of a donkey should be grey.

We were later to be told by a horsey gentleman who came to inspect her that he considered her to be of Arabian donkey stock.

'Look at the way she holds her head,' he said, 'she has the nobility of a thoroughbred.' Then he added, 'I've got a fancy she was bred for racing.'

We were impressed.

Neither Jeannie nor I understand the language of horsey people. We listen but cannot match it. Jeannie, when she was at the Savoy, listened a great deal to English, French and Irish talk about horses; jockeys, trainers and owners gave her advice, and once she won £50 on the Derby. Usually it was talk that was painfully forgotten.

Even to our eyes, however, Penny was a beautiful animal. Her head, when she was alerted by some noise or by some sight she did not understand, was elegantly intelligent with eyes sharp on the look-out and her large ears pointing inquisitively towards the mystery. After Penny came into our life we were never able to look at a horse without thinking how funny its ears looked.

On this particular morning, her first morning at Minack, Penny could not possibly have earned flattery from anyone.

We had moved her after breakfast from the lawn she had close cropped during the night to the stable meadow, so called because an ancient cowhouse and stable border one end of it. Here in early Spring, stretching towards the sea and in close view of the cottage, a variety of daffodil called Oliver Cromwell flowers profusely, defying the experts by doing so year after year without at any time receiving special attention. The bulbs have been in the ground for so long that I cannot find a person in the parish who can remember when they were planted.

A gentle slope falls to the end opposite the stables, then a stone hedge, and on the other side of it the big field which was our special pride when we first came to Minack. It was wasteland, covered in gorse and brambles, and gradually we brought it into cultivation until one year we grew four tons of potatoes. The field is called the cemetery field because in olden days dead cattle were buried at the bottom of it; and here at this point the field is poised above the cliff, the cliff which is cut into small meadows that fall steeply to the rocks and the sea of Mount's Bay.

On one side of the stable meadow is a finger of land which is the watercourse of the stream; lush in spring and summer with wild parsley, mint and watercress, it is in winter a haven for snipe. We do not allow anyone to shoot them.

On the other side is the path which leads down from the cottage to the cemetery field and the cliff. A low stone hedge divides it from the stable meadow, and it is a path which was in due course to give endless excitement to the donkeys.

Whenever they were in the stable meadow, and this was often, they would keep a watch as to who was passing by; and as soon as they caught sight of one of us they would race across the grass, then prance parallel to the hedge as we walked down the path until they reached the gap at the end where we had put a wooden fence.

Then, if we continued to walk on towards the cliff, there would be snorts and bellows, such a hullabaloo that we would be forced to turn back to talk to them. Often, in fact, we found it simpler to avoid the path and go across a field out of sight when we wanted to go down to the sea.

Here was Penny seeing the meadow for the first time and when I unfastened the halter, letting her be free, she looked around her for a moment, placidly without fear; and then began ravenously to eat the grass at her feet.

'That is the Dr Green Roy Teague talked about,' I murmured.

'We must get the vet as well,' said Jeannie.

There were bare patches on Penny, like moth-eaten patches on a discarded fur, and her coat was dull, like old silver waiting to be polished.

'No wonder she might have gone to the knacker's yard after the foal is born,' I said, 'she's scraggy, despite the foal.'

'I'll go and phone the vet straightaway.'

We had no telephone at the cottage, sure that by being without one we were spared complications that we could gladly do without. Thus, when we wanted to telephone, we either went to a call box two miles away or, when it was particularly urgent, asked permission to use the phone of our neighbour, Jack Cochram.

The vet was a Scotsman whom we had known for many years. A shy, polite man, he had the combined gifts of compassion and zeal which knighted his technical experience with a special quality. He was ready to make his skill available at any hour, there was never any suggestion that one might be wasting his time; and this attitude, together with that of his staff, induced many people to wish they were an animal instead of a human being.

The treatment he prescribed was simple if unpleasant. We had to rub her coat every other day for a fortnight with

53

a delousing powder.

'Do this,' he grinned, 'and let her eat as much grass as she wants. Then you'll find she'll be as right as rain when His Nibs arrives.'

He was always to call the foal 'His Nibs'.

'And when can we expect him?'

'In about three weeks. You'll go out into the field one day and find him beside her.'

'It seems very casual.'

'She'll prefer it that way.'

During the following fortnight we conscientiously carried out our instructions, helped by Penny who displayed no objection to the smelly powder with which we dusted her; and at the fortnight's end a stubble of hair had begun to cover the bare patches. But her coat was still dull, and her feet were awful. We were, in fact, filled with embarrassment when anyone asked to see her.

Her feet, particularly the two front ones, had the shape of Dutch clogs; and they were so long that she gave the impression that she walked on her heels. The cause of this was that the hooves of a donkey grow fast if they are not subjected to the wear of a hard surface; and so a donkey which does nothing else but graze all day requires a regular pedicure, performed by a blacksmith with a large file, a pair of clippers, and a strong arm with which to check any protest that the donkey concerned might try to make. It was the fear of this protest, and the fierce struggle that might ensue, which decided us to postpone Penny's pedicure until after the foal was born.

Penny, meanwhile, was oblivious there was anything in her appearance of which to be ashamed. It was clear by her gentle manner that she was exceedingly content. Here was grass galore, titbits which included carrots, apples, currant cakes and home-made bread, and a pair of humans who fussed over her as if she were a Queen. There was also a cat.

Lama's attitude was one of benign approval from her first sight of Penny. One might have expected upright fur and an arched back, a mood of anger or terror, when Penny like a moving mountain advanced towards her, a black cat so small that some people still mistook her for a kitten. Not a bit of it. There was not a quiver of a whisker nor a twitch of the tail. She was serenely confident that Penny threatened no harm.

This belief of Lama that nothing, not even a motor car, possessed any evil intentions towards her, frequently caused us alarm. How was it possible that the character of a cat could so change? Only three years before she was wild, and now nothing scared her. If a car came down the lane she lay in the middle until the car had to stop. If a dog lunged from a lead and barked insults, she complacently stared back, a Gandhi policy of non-violence. If a cat hater tried to avoid her, she pursued him with purrs. Once I saw a fox cub taking a look at her from a few yards off as she lay, a miniature Trafalgar lion, in the grass. When she became aware of his attention she got up, stretched and walked peacefully towards him. What does one do with a cat so trusting?

Soothing as it is to watch a creature so happy in its surroundings, there are some moments when the onlooker is scared stiff by its amiable antics. Penny was one day in the middle of the stable meadow munching away at the grass when I saw from the window the silky black figure of Lama advancing towards her. It was a deliberate, thoughtful advance because the grass was cat high, not high enough to advance in secret, not short enough to walk briskly through; indeed the grass was at that particular stage of growth when an intuitive, experienced cat leaps at one moment, then crawls at another. These alternate gestures brought her in due course to Penny's hind legs. They were powerful legs. They looked so powerful to me that, despite the nonchalant contentment Penny so apparently displayed, I quickly skirted them whenever I was having the fun of making a fuss of her. I respected the potential kick. I was not going to risk a sudden outburst of unreasonable, donkey temper. But Lama!

I watched her reach Penny, then frantically I called out to Jeannie. Lama, at that particular moment, was reaching a peak of her amiable confidence. And when Jeannie joined me I pointed to what was happening.

Lama was gently rubbing her head against one of Penny's hind legs; the loving, the embracing, the idiotic gesture of an idealist who had never been shocked into realism.

We held our breath as Penny continued to munch. Rub, rub, rub. First the head and the ears, then the cheek and the chin, even from a distance we could sense the ecstasy that Lama was enjoying.

'Shall I shout a warning?'

'Better not,' said Jeannie, 'or Penny might be startled into realizing what is happening.'

But Penny knew all the time who was there, and she didn't care. We saw her glance round, observe Lama for a second, then back again to her munching. And Lama continued her display of affection until suddenly she heard a rustle in the grass a little way off. Penny's hind leg was forgotten. A mouse was on the move. A more important task lay ahead than displaying her trust in a donkey.

We never tethered Penny again after her first night at Minack. We also learnt that it was even safe to take her for walks without a halter; and she would solemnly walk up the lane with us when we fetched the milk from the farm, requiring watchfulness on our part only when she passed a flower bed. Flowers, especially roses, had an irresistible attraction for her.

The third week went by without any hint of the foal and, as the news had now circulated that we possessed a donkey which was expecting, we were subjected to an

56

endless number of solicitous inquiries: 'Any news yet?'

In the middle of the fourth week we had taken Penny for a stroll before breakfast along one of the paths, and on returning to the cottage had put her in a small meadow near by. We then went in for our breakfast.

An hour or so later Jeannie went outside while I was at my desk writing a letter. Suddenly I heard her excited voice calling me. I dashed out of the door murmuring to myself: 'It's arrived!'

I nearly trod on Lama on the way, came face to face with a hissing Boris waddling up the path, and then in amazement saw why it was that Jeannie was calling for me.

A huge horse was standing in the small meadow with the donkey beside it.

'Good God,' I said, 'where has it come from?'

'Not the faintest idea.'

Our reaction was a mixture of merriment, irritation and concern. It was absurdly incongruous standing there, a giant of a horse, a chestnut, and it glared at us; while we in the meantime were smiling to ourselves at its funny little ears.

'What is it?' I asked cautiously, 'male or female?'

'A mare.'

'I'll dash up to the farm. Jack will know where she comes from.'

In due course the owner arrived, a very old man with watery eyes and a squeaky voice and no hat covering his bald head. I recognized him as a new arrival to the district, and owner of the cottages in one of which Jane Wyllie the young girl who used to work for us, once lived with her mother.

The mare took no notice of him except to edge away when he approached.

'Judy, Judy,' he coaxed on a high pitched note.

The mare replied by dashing through a gap in the hedge

which surrounded the meadow. She was out on her own now and into another. The old man was already out of breath but he bravely followed her.

'Judy, Judy.'

When the mare ignored him again, he turned to me.

'Bring the donkey out. It will quieten her down if she has the donkey with her.'

'Hell, I won't,' I said, 'that donkey is going to foal any time, any *moment*. I'm not going to bring her out within kicking distance of *your* monster.'

It was perhaps the harshness of this sentence that inspired the mare to take the violent action which now took place. She ignored the old man, thundered past him, then over a hedge and into the stable meadow. Over another hedge which I had thought unjumpable and then a dash down the lane. To my horror Jeannie was in her way. As soon as she had sensed there was going to be more trouble than we had expected, she had hastened to look for Lama. There she was, without having found Lama, bang in the way of the mare.

As if it were a circus trick, the mare jumped over her. And a few minutes later we watched the back of the old man panting up the lane, a galloping mare far far ahead and out of sight.

He caught her, we heard later, three miles away.

On the following Monday Jeannie and I and her mother, who was staying with us, went out for the day. When we returned to Minack, we met Jack Cochram who had been digging potatoes in his cliff which lies beyond the cottage. He had to pass the field in which we had left Penny.

He grinned when he saw us, a gay, amused grin.

'It's arrived!' he said happily, 'it's waiting for you!'

I have never gone down the lane so fast.

VIII

They were standing in the big field below the stable meadow, and beyond them the sun glinted on a still sea, disturbed only by the Stevenson fishing fleet out of Newlyn, their engines thumping, sailing like an Armada to distant fishing grounds.

Penny paused in her munching, strands of grass hanging out of her mouth, a proud mother no doubt, but still looking careworn, bare patches still on her back and her coat dull in the sunlight. The toy donkey huddled close to her, looking up at us inquisitively but without fear.

'It's so pretty I can't believe it's true!' laughed Jeannie.

'To think it might have gone to a circus!'

'Oh, Penny, you're a clever girl!'

We heard later from Jack Cochram that he had passed through the field at half-past eleven with his little girl, Janet, and Penny was on her own. There was a cloudburst shortly afterwards which continued for half an hour; and he came back across the field with a load of potatoes at half-past twelve. He looked towards Penny, and there was the foal.

'Look out,' I said, 'it's wobbling.'

It wobbled, lost its balance and collapsed on the grass. A ridiculous sight. All legs and fluffy brown coat, huge ears like old-fashioned motoring gloves, a tail like a fly whisk. I saw a comic eye, staring at me in surprise, and I had a feeling which made me smile, that it was furious. The indignity and the stupidity, just as it was introducing itself! It struggled, tiny hooves trying to get a grip on the grass, then a lurch, and it was upright again.

'What do you think it is?' I asked, 'boy or girl?'

'Shall we find out?'

'Well,' I said cautiously, 'it's a bit of a risk, isn't it? We haven't had any experience of this kind of thing.'

The little toy donkey now moved unsteadily under Penny who lifted her head from the grass and waited patiently while it had a drink of milk. The legs were like four match sticks propping a matchbox.

'I think it would be wiser,' I went on, 'if we asked Jack Cochram to investigate. Foals and calves are his business after all.'

'Seems a funny thing to have to ask him to do.'

'Might be funnier if we tried to find out ourselves.'

'I think you're a coward!'

'You said the other day if it were a girl you'd like to call her Marigold. You never mentioned what you'd call it if it were a boy.'

'Yes, I did,' said Jeannie, 'I thought we might call him Fred.'

Marigold or Fred. I looked at the unchristened creature who was now gazing thoughtfully back at me. Its nose was white like its mother's, and I noticed for the first time it had eye-lashes which were absurdly long. As I watched it took a few uncertain steps towards me, pushed its head forward, and gently nuzzled its nose in my hand. A sweet moment of trust.

'I think we had better get them up to the stables,' I said, 'the hay is spread on the floor.'

'Shall I carry the foal or will you?'

Jeannie was always so firm and yet so gentle when handling birds or animals. When she was a child she had wanted to be a vet, she had the patience and the quiet courage and the intuition to have made a successful one.

'You, of course,' I said, 'if it's not too heavy.'

Too heavy! She picked up Marigold or Fred as easily as if it had been an Alsatian puppy, holding it in her arms with its head drooping over her shoulder, and off we went across the field, then up the path to the stables. It was a gay procession. Jeannie leading the way murmuring sweet nothings to the foal, Penny in the middle snatching at succulent grasses as she passed them, exuding pride in her achievement, supremely confident that Jeannie ahead of her was taking her foal to safety. Here was her home. Nothing to fear now. Here at last was the foal she had carried with her on her journeys from Ireland, there in front of her, on the way to a warm stable, and time lay ahead together.

As for myself, as I walked up the path behind them, I was pondering on the value of the moment. Had we ignored the call of the telegram, had we taken the night train to London, we would have returned to Minack with memories of many faces, lunches in hot restaurants, late nights and thirsty mornings, packed tubes and rushing taxis, a vast spending of money, much noise, and yet a feeling of satisfaction that we had at last pushed ourselves again into the circle of sophisticated pleasure; and it was over. Instead we possessed two donkeys; and the magic of this moment.

It is a sickness of this mid-twentieth century that the basic virtues are publicized as dull. The arbiters of this age, finding it profitable to destroy, decree from the heights that love and trust and loyalty are suspect qualities; and to sneer and be vicious, to attack anyone or any cause which possesses roots, to laugh at those who cannot defend themselves, are the aims to pursue. Their ideas permeate those who only look but do not think. Jokes and debating points, however unfair, are hailed as fine entertainment. Truth, by this means, becomes unfashionable, and its value is measured only by the extent it can be twisted. And yet nothing has changed since the beginning. Truth is the only weapon that can give the soul its freedom.

As we reached the stables I had a sudden sense of great happiness, foolish, childish, spontaneous like the way I felt when my parents visited me at school. Free from dissection. Unexplainable by logic. Here were these two animals which were useless from a material point of view, destined to add chains to our life, and yet reflecting the truth that at this instant sent my heart soaring.

'Do you realize, Jeannie,' I said, after we had put them safely in the stable and were leaning over the stable door watching them, 'that people would laugh at us for being sentimental idiots?'

'Of course I do. Some would also be angry.'

'Why?'

'They are afraid.'

'Of what?'

'Of facing up to the fact they are incapable of loving anything or anyone except themselves.'

Guerrilla warfare continues ceaselessly between those who love animals and those who believe the loving is grossly overdone. Animals, in the view of some people, can contribute nothing to the brittle future of our computer civilization, and therefore to love them or to care for them is a decadent act. Other people consider that in a world in which individualism is a declining status, an animal reflects their own wish to be free. These people also love an animal for its loyalty. They sometimes feel that their fellow human beings are so absorbed by their self survival that loyalty is considered a liability in the pursuit of material ambition. Animals, on the other hand, can bestow dependable affection and loyalty on all those who wish to receive it.

'It's odd in any case,' I said, 'that whenever one uses the word sentimental it sounds like an insult. Sentimental, before it became a coin of the sophisticated, described a virtue.'

'In what way?'

'It described kindness.'

'Surely in excess?'

'Only later, in the Victorian age. In those days people

were nauseating in the way they fussed over animals, and this was reflected in those awful pictures we all know. Such an over-flow of sickly superficiality became a middle-class curse to avoid. Animal haters like to keep alive the idea that Victorian sentiment is synonymous with animal loving. It eases their consciences.'

'Anyhow, I'm sentimental,' said Jeannie, 'and I see no reason why I should be ashamed of it. I only wish human beings were as giving as animals.'

'Don't be so cynical!'

'Well you know what I mean. Human beings can be so petty and mean and envious. You can't say they are progressing in themselves as fast as the new machines they're producing.'

'That's true.'

'One can rely on animals to give kindness when one needs it most.'

'One has naturalness from animals and one is inclined to expect the same from human beings.'

'And by that you mean we expect too much?'

'Yes. Animals do not have income tax, status symbols, bosses breathing down their necks.'

Penny came and pushed her nose at us over the door and below her, so that we had to lean over and stretch out an arm to touch it, was the absurd little foal.

'Anyhow,' I said, 'I'm now very glad we've given a home to these two. They will amuse us, annoy us in a humorous way, trust us, and give others a great deal of pleasure.'

'Silly things,' said Jeannie, smiling.

'And so let's be practical. Let's find Jack, and ask him to discover whether we have Marigold or Fred.'

Jack Cochram, dark with wiry good looks, looked like a Cornishman but was born a Londoner. He was evacuated to Cornwall during the war, and has remained here ever since. His farm has fields spread round Minack, and he and his partner Walter Grose were neighbours who were always ready to help. Walter lived at St Buryan and came to the farm every day. Jack and his wife lived with their children Susan and Janet in the farmhouse at the top of Minack lane, an old stone-built farmhouse with windows facing across the fields towards Mount's Bay.

After a while in the stable Penny had made it quite plain that she wanted to move, and so we had taken her, Jeannie carrying the foal again, to the little three-cornered meadow where she had had her encounter with the mare. It was close to the cottage and we could keep an eye on them both.

An hour later Jack Cochram arrived, and unfortunately I had been called away. Jeannie therefore led Jack to the meadow and showed him the foal on the other side of the barrier I had erected at the entrance. Jeannie said afterwards that as they stood there, Penny stared suspiciously at them. This was the first time a stranger had seen her foal, and she was on guard. It would have been wiser, therefore, had they waited, allowing Penny to become accustomed to Jack; or if Jeannie had fetched her a handful of carrots to bribe her into being quiet. But Jeannie had been lulled by Penny's previous serenity, her placid nature, and she failed to understand that Penny might believe her foal was about to be stolen. Jack, in his kindness, jumped over the barrier, picked up the foal, and immediately faced pandemonium.

Jeannie was terrified. She saw Penny rear up, bare her teeth, then advance on her hind legs towards Jack while pawing the air like an enraged boxer with her front legs. Jack quickly put the foal to the ground, but by this time Penny was in such a temper that she failed to see it, and she knocked it flat as she went for Jack. When she reached him she was screaming like a hyena, and he was standing with his back to a broken-down wall in a corner of the meadow. He put up an arm above his head as she attacked him, trying to punch his way clear; and then, seizing a split

66

second, and also swearing I am sure never to investigate the sex of a donkey again, he jumped over the barrier to safety.

Jeannie, meanwhile, was in the meadow herself, kneeling beside the foal which was lying on its side, eyes shut, tongue out and breathing in gasps. She knelt there stroking its head, Penny somewhere behind her calm again, and thought it was dying. Then she heard Jack cheerfully call to her, unperturbed by his experience: 'It's a girl!'

She told me later that Marigold, at this exact moment, opened an eye and flickered an eyelash. Jeannie said it looked so bewitching that she bent down and kissed it at which Marigold gave a deep sigh. Then a few minutes later she struggled to her feet and sturdily went over to Penny who licked her face, then waited as she had a drink of milk. When Jeannie left them they were standing together; and they may well have been laughing together. They had reason to do so.

When our friend, the vet, arrived early in the afternoon, and after we had toasted the health and happiness of Marigold, we learnt that Jack had made a mistake.

Marigold was Fred.

IX

Jeannie's mother was staying with us when Fred was born, and she was a participant in his first escapade. She it was who had connived with Jeannie to defeat my then anti-cat attitude by introducing Monty into our London household when he was a kitten; and now the happiness that Monty gave us, first in London and then at Minack, was to be repaid in part in the few months to come by Fred. Fred captured her heart from the first moment she saw him; and when she left Minack to return to her home, she waited expectantly for our regular reports on his activities.

He was inquisitive, cheeky, endearing, from the beginning; and we soon discovered he had a sense of humour which he displayed outrageously whenever his antics had embroiled him in trouble. A disarming sense of humour; a device to secure quick forgiveness, a comic turn of tossing his head and putting back his floppy ears, then grinning at us, prancing meanwhile, giving us the message: 'I know I've been naughty, but isn't it FUN?'

He was a week old when he had this first escapade, a diversion, a mischievous exploration into tasting foal-like independence. Perhaps his idea was to prove to us that he could now walk without wobbling, that he was a sturdy baby donkey who could dispense with the indignity of being carried from one place to another. If this was so it was a gesture that was over-ambitious; and though the result caused us much laughter, Penny on the other hand was distraught with alarm at her son's idiotic bravado.

I had guarded the open side of the little yard in front of the stables, the side which joined the space in front of the cottage, with a miscellaneous collection of wooden boxes, a couple of old planks, and a half-dozen trestles which during the daffodil season supported the bunching tables. It may have been a ramshackle barrier but I certainly thought it good enough to prevent any excursions by the donkeys, and in particular by Fred. I had omitted, however, to take into account that there was a gap between the legs of one of the trestles suitably large enough for an intelligent foal to skip through. Suitably large enough? It was the size of half the windscreen of a small car, and only after the escape had been made could I condemn myself for making a mistake.

The first to be startled by what had happened was Jeannie's mother who was sitting on the white seat beside the verbena bush reading a newspaper. She was absorbed by some story, when suddenly the paper was bashed in her face.

'Good heavens,' she said, 'Fred! You cheeky thing!'

She explained afterwards that Fred appeared as surprised as herself by what he had done, though he quickly recovered himself, danced a little fandango, then set off like a miniature Derby runner down the lane in the direction of Monty's Leap. Meanwhile there had developed such a commotion in the yard behind the barrier, where Penny was snorting, whinnying and driving herself like a bulldozer at the trestles, that Jeannie and I, who were in the cottage, rushed out to see what was happening.

We were in time to see Fred waver on his course, appear to stumble, then fall headlong into a flower bed.

'My geraniums!' cried Jeannie. The reflex cry of the gardener. Only flowers are hurt.

'Idiot!' I said.

Penny by now was frantic and as I dashed down the path I saw that the battering ram of her shoulders was just about to break a way clear for her. I left Jeannie to join her mother who had already reached Fred, and set about calming a rampaging donkey which looked prepared to eat me if I gave her a chance. A minute later Fred appeared in Jeannie's arms.

'Not a scratch as far as we can see, and thoroughly ashamed. Aren't you, Fred?'

He had grown so fast in a week that Jeannie could no longer carry him, as she did at the beginning, like a puppy. It was an effort to hold him, and his legs dangled close to the ground.

But he did not look ashamed to me. For here was the common denominator of all things young, the foolishness of enterprise before it is ready, the gusto of such foolishness, the bruised vanity after being found out, the genius of making the error appear inconsequential.

I moved a trestle, shielding it against Penny so that Jeannie could drop Fred in the gap without fear of attack from his hysterical mother. She *was* hysterical. She was like a wild beast in her distress.

'There you are, Penny,' said Jeannie, putting Fred to the ground and pushing him through the gap, 'nothing to worry about.'

I fancy that Fred expected a joyous reunion, a pat on the back for being so original as to attack a newspaper, to startle an elderly lady, to cause consternation within a week of his arrival. He was mistaken. Penny was as angry as she was relieved at being united with Fred; and she chased him. She chased him with her nose, chastising his buttocks with her soft white nose as if for the moment she considered it a whip. She chased him round the yard and into the stable, and out again. She was so furious that she wanted to teach him a lesson he would never forget. Not on our behalf, but on hers.

Fred's reaction seemed to be a relish that he was loved on both sides of the barrier, a wonderful hint that if the imponderables went well, he would for ever and for ever have the most wonderful life imaginable. And so when Penny's fury had subsided, when Fred found himself once again a young donkey freed from his mother's strictures, he smiled, putting his ears back and shaking his head. I am certain he was saying that he enjoyed every minute of his escape, the fall didn't matter, life was fun and mistakes didn't count so long as there were years ahead in which to correct them. I feel sure that when he came rushing up to my hand which I held out to him, nuzzling it with his nose, he was telling me what a hilarious time lay ahead of us.

'I have a feeling,' said Jeannie's mother later, 'that this donkey is going to be a nuisance!'

She did not mean, of course, this to be a reproach. Nor for that matter a warning. It was a gentle joke, said in a soft voice with just the trace of a Scottish accent. I realize in retrospect that her affection for Fred stemmed from something deeper than a superficial enchantment for a Disney-like creature. He was to her, in the last few months of her life, a link with the future. Her intuition made her aware that time was against her, and so she was glad to find in this absurd little donkey a bridge. Jeannie's uncle told Jeannie how a few weeks later he was with her mother waiting for a bus to take them from Gloucester Road to Hyde Park corner. They waited twenty minutes at the bus stop, not because there were no buses. Three went by; but Jeannie's mother went on talking, and the subject was Fred. The poor man cursed the donkey as he stood there, listening patiently. He did not know the secret. Fred, at that very instant, running free on the Cornish cliffs, the skies and wild winds, sunny days and torrential rain, the sea lurching then calm, scents of the salt, wild grasses, pinks, meadow sweet, puzzling cries of gulls, woodpeckers laughing, badgers solidly plodding ageless paths, foxes alert, exultant chorus of the early morning, marsh warblers, summer larks, blackbirds trumpeting, wrens erupting; for all these Fred was the spokesman. These pleasures, enriched by the eyes and ears of centuries, projecting the kindness of permanence and security, dwelt there hopefully in her mind.

And there were the incidents of which she had been a witness at Minack. Visits at daffodil time and potato time, Jeannie coming into the packing shed with baskets of flowers in either hand, Jeannie in shorts under a blazing sun grubbing through the soil quicker than anyone as she picked up the potatoes. Glorious moments of anticipation when arriving for Christmas, carefully thought-out presents in gaily coloured paper awaiting disclosure, champagne on the day – shall we have the turkey for lunch or for dinner? Times of disaster when gales and salt spray cut the potato tops like a scimitar, leaving a barren harvest in their wake; and a terrible spring when a disease attacked the daffodils, spotting the petals with a brown mould, making them useless for market so that the compost heap grew higher and higher with thrown-away stems. She had been at Minack when Lama was first seen, a black spot in a meadow, and when Monty died. She had known Jane and Shelagh of *A Drake at the Door* when each had first arrived, Jane with the corn-coloured hair touching her shoulders, Shelagh with the shy smile, both with the gift of making us feel happy that they were with us. Funny times . . . she was in the cottage on Jeannie's birthday when, after a night of raging wind, I went out to find the cloches scattered across their field. I was fighting in the gale to save those which were left when suddenly I saw Jeannie, struggling towards me. 'A cup of tea with Glucose,' she shouted above the noise. I was grateful she had taken pity on me, and I seized the cup and took a gulp. It tasted like acid. 'Hell,' I shouted, 'have you poisoned me?' When I got back to the cottage her mother was waiting at the doorway. 'Look dear,' she said gently, 'you opened the tin of Epsom salts.' Quiet times, when there was the idleness of a deck chair in the wood, or a stroll to the cliff to watch the little fishing boats feathering for mackerel and the big ones on their way to and from Newlyn. Or just sitting on the white seat where Fred bashed the newspaper.

A month after she had returned to London, and Jeannie was with her, I took a pair of scissors and cut a small piece of Fred's mane and sent it to her tied with a pale blue ribbon. It was still in her handbag eight months later when she died.

'Whatever else he does in his life,' said Jeannie thoughtfully, 'Fred has justified his existence.'

X

Fred now faced a glorious summer of adulation. Nobody could resist him. Children and grown ups both uttered cries of delight as soon as they saw his gambolling fluffy figure, cameras were poised, small hands held out to stroke him, picnic baskets searched for sugar; and his response was to pander to his admirers in various fetching ways. Sometimes he would stand beside them soulfully staring into the distance as they stroked him, sometimes he would surprise a new admirer by a comical, harmless dance, sometimes he would show off his speed by sprinting across the meadow, sometimes he would hug close to Penny, but always sooner or later he would allow every admirer to fondle him.

Jeannie and I soon found that his presence was exceedingly helpful. When one writes about the place where one lives, it is to be expected that strangers will call. Seldom a day passed in the summer without someone arriving at Minack; and as we were so far off the beaten track it was a feat of exploration to have found us.

Visitors were of all ages and came from all parts of the country. The snag of these visits was that we were always caught by surprise. We would have to emerge from a greenhouse in which we had been tending tomatoes, and appear in the role of host and hostess with our hands and faces green with the juice of the leaves. Or we would be disturbed at some peak time when we were wanting to rush something into Penzance. One daffodil time a couple arrived as we were packing our flower boxes as fast as we could into the Land-Rover so that we could catch the flower train to London. We also knew that we were far behind in our picking, and there was a whole meadow awaiting our urgent attention. I suggested to the couple that they might like to see such a beautiful sight, and off they went. When they returned, the woman in a lofty voice said: 'I would have thought you would have found time to pick those daffodils!' Jeannie had to stop me from braining her.

Once we had a visitor who looked up at the gull on the roof and asked: 'Is it plastic?' There was a man who arrived on a bicycle and, pointing to the pedometer on the front wheel, said: 'I've ridden three hundred and seventy miles to prove to my wife that you are not fictitious!' Another time we had a car load of people whose car got stuck at Monty's Leap, the low slung chassis was jammed on the bed of the stream; they were there for four hours. We have had strangers who have brought us presents. We frequently met people with whom afterwards we kept in touch; and at all times Jeannie and I found it a wonderfully rewarding experience that any of these people had taken the trouble to find their way to Minack.

Such visits, however, inevitably took time because we could not just say hello and good-bye. Tasks we were performing had to be suspended and, if they were tedious tasks like hand weeding the freesia beds, we often found it difficult to return to them. The nature of the visit was likely to have disturbed our sense of routine, and we were inclined to relax and await the possible arrival of another visitor.

Our usual procedure was first to show these visitors the gull on the roof, provided one of the gulls was there; but it was maddening how often Knocker, Squeaker or Peter would let us down, and would only sail into view after the visitors had disappeared up the lane. Boris, the drake, however, could always be relied upon. He enjoyed attention as long as no one tried to touch him. He squatted imperiously in the shade of the flower house or in the grass by the elms, eyeing the strangers, stretching his neck forward towards them, hissing gently at them if they seemed to be coming too close, hissing loudly if they did and at the same time raising the feathers on the top of his head as a cat will lift its fur in anger. Then he would rise majestically to his large yellow webbed feet and waddle away, waggling his olive green tail feathers in protest.

Lama's behaviour, as one might expect, was unpredictable. Sometimes she was in a sociable mood and she would appear jauntily with a hop, skip and miaow. At other times she would remain obstinately in her hiding places while we rushed round the usual sites bleating for her. At last the visitor would say: 'Don't bother to look any more. It doesn't matter. We didn't come specially to see her.' Then, of course, Lama in a trice would be with us.

There were many occasions, however, when people did come specially to see her. Her particular attraction was that she had been a wild cat; a cat who had spent extreme youth in the cold but now was conquered by comfort, an irresistible situation for cat admirers, a cat who had been tamed, a human victory over the feline species. Jeannie and I, on these occasions, would anxiously watch how she would behave because there was one thing she loathed and that was sugary flattery. Any visitor who tried to win her that way was beneath her contempt. Hence if someone began cooing at her in the manner so often adopted towards cats, Lama would stiffen in disgust. I have often seen her in the arms of a visitor who was cooing like mad, have seen the danger signal, then leapt forward and snatched her away a split second before harm was done.

The presence of the donkeys now produced a major diversion. Sometimes I had found a conversation difficult to sustain and I would stare out to sea, the visitor beside me, murmuring foolishly over and over again: 'Isn't it a glorious view?' There was now no fear of a faltering conversation, no cause for me to fill a silence with an inane remark. The shyest visitor was filled with rapturous excitement as soon as I said: 'Have you ever seen a baby donkey?'

I thereupon led the way to the meadow, and it was usually the stable meadow, where Penny and Fred were perusing the green grass around them.

'Penny! Fred!' I would call out authoritatively, as if it were the most natural thing in the world for them immediately to obey me.

'Penny! Fred!'

They would stare from afar and make no move.

'Come on, Penny!' I would shout again, wanting to prove to my visitors that I was in command. 'COME ON!'

I soon noticed, before he was even a month old, that Fred was usually the first to react. He could be in deep slumber, lying flat on the ground with Penny standing on guard beside him; but when I called he would wake up, raise his head in query, scramble to his feet, pause while looking in my direction, then advance towards me. First a walk, then a scamper.

'He's a very intelligent donkey,' I would then say proudly. A sop to the fact that Penny had ignored me.

But Penny at this time was still a sorry sight, the sores had gone but her coat was still thin. We had to excuse her appearance by repeating the story of how we had found her. We explained her elongated feet by telling how we had waited for Fred to be born before dealing with them, and that now we were waiting for the blacksmith. We chattered on with our excuses and then realized no one was listening. All anyone wanted to do was to fuss over Fred.

'Aren't his ears huge?'

'I love his nose.'

'Look at his feet! Like a ballet dancer's!'

'What eyelashes!'

'Does he hee-haw?'

I remember both his first hee-haw and his first buttercup. He was a week old when he decided to copy his grazing mother, putting his nose to the grass without quite knowing what was expected of him. He roamed beside her sniffing importantly this grass and that; and then suddenly he saw the buttercup. A moment later he came scampering towards me with the buttercup sticking out of the corner of his mouth like a cigarette, and written all over his ridiculous face was: 'Look what I've found!'

The first hee-haw was to occur one afternoon in the autumn when Jeannie and I were weeding the garden. There was no apparent reason to prompt it. They were not far away from us in the meadow, and every now and then we had turned to watch them contentedly mooching around. And then came the sound.

It was at first like someone's maiden attempt to extract a note from a saxophone. It was a gasping moan. It then wavered a little, began to gain strength and confidence, started to rise in the scale, and then suddenly blossomed into a frenzied hiccuping tenor-like crescendo.

'Heavens,' I said, 'what an excruciating noise!'

'Fred!' called out Jeannie, laughing, 'what on earth's the matter?'

At this moment we saw Penny lifting up her head to the sky. And out of her mouth came the unladylike noise which we had already learnt to expect. No bold brassy hee-haw from her. It was a wheezy groan which at intervals went into a falsetto. Here was a donkey, it seemed, who longed to hee-haw but couldn't. All she could do was to struggle out inhuman noises as her contribution to the duet. It was painful not only to listen to, but also to watch. This was donkey frustration. The terrible trumpet of her son had reawakened ambitions. She wanted to compete with him, but she hadn't a ghost of a chance.

Meanwhile, as the summer advanced, Penny had developed a role of her own towards the visitors. She was clearly, for instance, used to children and although it was Fred who received the initial caressing attention it was

81

Penny, because she was full grown, who only could give them a ride. Ignored during the first ten minutes, she then became a Queen in importance, and she would patiently allow a child to be hoisted on her back, and a ride would begin.

But Jeannie and I soon found that her job was far easier, far less exhausting than ours. One of us had to lead Penny by a halter, and as she would not move without Fred, Fred had to be led along as well. I had bought him a smart halter of white webbing within a few days of his being born, and he never resented wearing it. He wore it as if it were a decoration, a criss-cross of white against his fluffy brown coat giving him an air of importance. One visitor said he reminded her of a small boy who was allowed to wear trousers when all his friends were still wearing shorts.

Up and down the meadow we walked and all the while we had to be on guard against accidents. We had a nightmarish fear that a child might fall off and so while one of us led the donkeys, the other walked alongside holding the rider. We spent hours that summer in this fashion.

There was no doubt, therefore, that the presence of the donkeys was a huge success. People who had come to see Jeannie and me went away happy because they had met Penny and Fred.

'The donkeys have *made* our day,' said two strangers who had driven specially from a distance to call on us.

And there were other occasions when I sauntered out of the cottage on seeing strangers draw up in a car, a bright smile on my face.

'May we,' an eager voice would ask from the car window, 'see the donkeys?'

XI

An eloquent feature of the donkeys was their stare; and we never succeeded in growing accustomed to it. It was a weapon they used in morose moments of displeasure. There they would stand side by side in a meadow steadfastly watching us, exuding disapproval, condemning us for going about our business and not theirs.

The stare increased in its frequency after the summer and the visitors had disappeared; for Fred, by this time, expected attention like a precocious child film star who believes that adulation goes on for ever. He missed the applause, lumps of sugar, and posing for his picture. He was a Prince without courtiers. He was at a loss as to how to fill his day. So he would stare, and hope that we would fill the gap.

'Why can't we go to another meadow?'

'I'd like a walk.'

'Oh dear, what *is* there to do?'

And when finally we relented, yielding to the influence of the stare, and dropped whatever we were doing, and decided to entertain him, Fred would look knowingly at Penny.

'Here they come, Mum. We've done it.'

Penny's stare was prompted by a more practical reason. True she enjoyed diversions but they were not an innocent necessity as they were for Fred. She was old enough in experience to be phlegmatic, her role as a donkey was understood; she had to be patient, enduring the contrariness of human beings, surprised by the affection she was now suddenly receiving, and yet prepared it might end with equal suddenness. She didn't have to be amused. All she had to remember was to have enough milk for Fred, and that the grass was losing its bite. Her stare was to induce us to change to another meadow or to take her for a walk, not for the exercise, but for the grasses and weeds of the hedgerows. A walk to her was like a stroll through a cafeteria.

It did not take much to amuse Fred. He liked, for instance, the simple game of being chased, although he and I developed together certain nuances that the ordinary beholder might not have noticed. There was the straightforward chase in which I ran round a meadow panting at his heels, Penny watching us with an air of condescension, and Fred cantering with the class of a potential racehorse; there was a variation in which I chased them both, aiming to separate them by corralling one or other in a corner. This caused huge excitement when my mission had succeeded with Penny in a corner and Fred the odd man out. He would nuzzle his nose into my back, then try to break through my outstretched arms, snorting, putting his head down with his ears flat, and giving the clear impression he was laughing uproariously.

He loved to be stalked. In a meadow where the grass was high I would go down on my hands and knees and move my way secretly towards him. Of course he knew I was coming. He would be standing a few yards off, ears pricked, his alert intelligent face watching the waving grass until, at the mutually agreed moment, I would make a mock dash at him; and he would make an equally mock galloping escape. This was repeated again and again until I, with my knees bruised and out of breath, called it a day.

I think, though, that our most hilarious game was that of the running flag. I would get over the hedge to the meadow or field he was in, then run along the other side holding a stick with a cloth attached high enough for him to see it. It baffled him. It maddened him. He would race along parallel to unseen me whinnying in excitement; and when, to titillate his puzzlement, I would stop, bring the stick down, so suddenly he saw nothing, nine times out of ten he would rend the air with hee-haws. Of course he knew all the while that it was a pretence; and when I jumped back over the hedge to join him he greeted me with the cavorting of an obviously happy donkey.

These were deliberate games. There were others which came by chance. Electricity had at last come to the cottage and on one occasion I saw a Board Inspector running across the field with a joyous Fred close behind him. The Inspector, I am sure, was glad when he reached the pole he had come to inspect, and could speedily climb out of reach.

It was a fact that Fred enjoyed the chase as much as being chased. He was fascinated, for instance, by Lama and Boris. As soon as he saw the little black cat he would put his head down, move towards her, struggling to free himself from the halter with which I was holding him. Or if Lama had entered the meadow in which he was roaming, his boredom would immediately vanish. Why is she here? How fast can she run? Let me see if I can catch her.

And yet I never saw any evidence that there was viciousness in his interest. Lama, because of her trust in all men and things, gave him plenty of opportunities to show the truth of his intent; and his intent seemed only to chase to play. It was the same with Boris. On one occasion Fred escaped from his halter, saw Boris a few yards from him and, head down close to white feathered tail, proceeded to chase Boris round the large static greenhouse in front of the cottage. The waddle and the hiss of Boris was distressing to behold and to hear, but I found myself watching without fear that Fred might do any harm. It was clear that Fred was only nudging him. Here is my nose, there your tail. Go a little faster, old drake.

The donkeys now spent much of their time in the field adjoining the cottage, and it was here that Fred had his first major fright. The field was so placed that the stare could be imposed upon us in a particularly effective fashion. It was a large field sloping downwards to the wood with a corner which was poised shoulder high above the tiny garden. Hence when the donkeys came to this corner, which was often, they looked down at us. They could even see into the cottage.

'The donkeys are wanting attention,' Jeannie would say as she sat in a chair by the fire, 'shall I deal with them or will you?'

There were other occasions when they chose to stand in the corner purely, I am sure, to emphasize the toughness of their lot. When there was a storm with rain beating down on the roof and the wind rattling the windows they would stand in view of our comfort. Two miserable donkeys who could easily have found shelter under a hedge. Two waifs. Fred with his fluffy coat bedraggled and flattened against his body like a small boy's hair after a bathe. Penny, years of storm suffering behind her, her now shiny black coat unaffected, passing on her experience to Fred

'Put your head down, son. The rain will run off your nose.'

But the day that Fred had his fright was sunny and still, an October day of Indian summer and burnished colours, the scent of the sea touching the falling leaves, no sadness in the day. Fred, now a colt not a foal, was enjoying himself grazing beside Penny, nibbling the grass like a grown up, when under the barbed wire that closed the gap at the top of the field rushed a boxer.

Had Boris and Lama witnessed what followed no doubt they would have laughed to themselves . . . a taste of his own medicine . . . that is how *we* feel when he comes thundering after us. The difference, however, was that the boxer was savage. It chased Fred as if it were intent on the kill. It had the wild hysteria of a mad wolf. It ignored the galloping hooves. It tried to jump on Fred's back, teeth bared, its ugly face ablaze with primitive fury. And all the while Fred raced round and round the field bellowing his terror like a baby elephant pursued by a tiger.

I had arrived on the scene at the double to find Jeannie already there running after the dog with Penny trumpeting beside her; and a man walking unconcernedly across the field towards the cottage. The contrast between calm and chaos was startling.

'I have lost my way,' said the man when he saw me, 'can you direct me to Lamorna?'

His nonchalance astounded me. My temper was alight.

'Is that your dog?' I shouted back.

'Yes,' he smiled, 'he's having a good time.'

'GOOD TIME? What the hell are you saying? Look at that baby donkey, look at your dog!' I was incoherent with rage. I raised my arm and wanted to hit him. 'How dare you come through private property without a dog like that on a lead!'

'He doesn't like a lead.'

It was fortunate that at this precise moment I saw that the boxer had broken away from the chase, that Jeannie, after a moment's soothing of Fred, was hastening to my support. The sight restrained me.

'Get that dog, then get off my land!'

Even this was not the end of it. Indifferent to my anger, oblivious that Jeannie had now joined in the attack, he took the dog by the scruff of the neck and began to climb down into the garden from the point where the donkeys liked to stand.

'Not that way!'

I had visions of the dog breaking free, and indulging his stupidity by wringing the necks of Lama and Boris.

'But I want to get to Lamorna,' said the man plaintively, 'and surely I can go up that lane?'

'You can't, and that's that. You can go back to wherever you came from, and go quick!'

It always surprises me why so many dog owners are dull minded. They thrust the bad manners of their dogs upon the rest of us. They ignore the possibility of damage that dogs can inflict. They are deaf. I have known a dog which would bark for two hours on end, its owner close by insensitive to the people miles around who were cursing. I like dogs. I only blame their owners. I might even have liked the boxer.

The attachment between Penny and Fred was intense. If a gate was shut and Penny was one side of it, Fred the other, both would show signs of great distress. There was never any question of taking them out each on their own. In the meadows they were always within a few yards of each other; and when Fred lay down for a sleep, Penny would stand guard beside him.

Fred was always particularly perturbed by Penny's six-weekly pedicure. Along would come the blacksmith armed with a massive pair of cutters and a large file, and Penny would be ushered into the stables while Fred remained outside. He was certain something awful was happening to his mother, and this was not helped by the tantrums Penny sometimes displayed. On one side of the stable door the blacksmith was holding the leg of a plunging Penny; on the other, Fred was behaving as if he were never going to see her again.

These should have been signs enough to put Jeannie and me on our guard. The uncontrollable affection was a potential explosion. We only had to provide the opportunity, by testing it to breaking point, for a situation to arise in which someone was hurt. And this is exactly what happened.

We decided one evening to take the donkeys for a walk up the lane, and into a field which led through the top end of our wood. Jeannie, because she has always maintained a wondrous, innocent, totally trusting attitude towards the behaviour of all animals, was not only riding Penny but carrying Lama as well. She had done it a number of times before. She held the rope of the halter as a single-sided rein while a comfortable Lama sat snugly with her two front paws around Penny's mane. Lama enjoyed it, Penny displayed no objection while I, though appreciating the pleasant sight of cat, donkey and my pretty wife, also viewed the whole affair with a tolerant suspicion. It seemed to be asking for trouble. My weakness, however, was that I did not feel strongly enough about this to complain.

We were in the field and were on the way back, a pastoral scene. Jeannie in pink pants astride Penny, Lama beatific and merging into Penny's glossy coat. Fred and I a few yards ahead. Nothing untoward seemed about to happen. We were all enjoying ourselves. Jeannie was telling me that Lama was purring, Penny was pausing at intervals to snatch a mouthful of grass, Fred wearing his bright, white halter was taking a great interest in all around. Why this? What's that? In every glance one sensed the gay inquisitiveness of the very young.

Fred and I reached the open gateway of the field, then turned right down the sloping lane leading for the cottage. It was, on my part, a thoughtless mistake. I was so amused by the way Fred was enjoying himself, leading me by his halter instead of me leading him, that I never thought of waiting for Jeannie. The setting was too normal and peaceful for me to imagine that Penny might panic when Fred disappeared out of her sight.

Suddenly I heard Jeannie shout. Then I saw Penny come out of the field at the gallop, jump a ditch, and in an instant she was dashing towards me. Her head was down, she looked wild, and had she been by herself I would have jumped aside and let her race on. But to my horror Jeannie was still astride her, vainly trying to grip with her legs . . . for in her hands she held Lama.

She said afterwards that her only concern was to save Lama. Lama, she visioned, would be trampled on. Lama

91

was the only one in danger, not herself. But for me who was standing there in her path, a flash of my life which seemed an eternity, her fall at speed to the granite based, jagged stone surface of the lane was inevitable. Lama, as far as I was concerned, could look after herself.

Jeannie was slipping to the side on my right. She was silent, no calling out for help.

'I'm going to the right,' I shouted.

My instinct was to try to catch her, cowboy fashion, taking her as she fell, leaving Penny to gallop on. I let Fred go and held out my arms.

I do not now think I had a chance to succeed. Penny was moving too fast, too heavy for me to check her, and indeed the very fact that I was standing there made her swerve as she reached me; and that was the moment when Jeannie fell.

My right hand seemed to clasp her for a brief instant, and then I was buffeted as Penny raced past me. The sound of the hooves disappeared. Incongruously I was aware of a lark singing. A rattle of a tractor came from a distance. All was normal again, quiet and peaceful and pastoral, as it had been five minutes before.

I knelt down beside Jeannie, quite still and eyes shut, and cupped her head in my hands.

XII

Jeannie was unconscious for three or four minutes, and I was at a loss to know whether to stay with her or leave her and hurry for help. I took off my jersey and made it a pillow under her head. And I had just decided to rush up to the farm, when she opened her eyes.

'Where's Lama?' she murmured.

Hell, I said to myself, here I am frantic with worry and all she thinks of is Lama.

'Lama's all right,' I said soothingly, 'what about you?'

As it happened I hadn't a notion what had happened to Lama. I remembered that as Jeannie fell she flung Lama forward so that Lama flew past me like a small black football. Then she disappeared into the pandemonium of Penny's gallop.

The fact, however, that Jeannie had spoken sent bells ringing through me. The question of Lama could wait, so also the whereabouts of the donkeys.

'I had better get you to hospital.'

'No fear.'

'Come on, no argument, please.'

I was delighted, of course, that she did choose to argue. Here was the good sign. The bossy, if faint, contradiction. Her injury could not be serious.

I helped her to her feet and I walked with her leaning on me, slowly back to the cottage.

'Please don't take me to hospital.'

Her chin was cut and bleeding.

'All right,' I said, thankful for the alertness she was showing, 'we'll compromise. We'll see if we can find an off-duty doctor.'

We had reached Monty's Leap. A few yards further on there was a grass verge, just big enough for us to park the Land-Rover sometimes during the daffodil season. It was opposite that section of the stables we used as a packing shed.

'Now look . . .' And I couldn't help smiling.

'Donkeys!' said Jeannie. And she too smiled.

Two shamefaced donkeys. Halters still harnessing their heads, the ropes dragging the ground. They stood there waiting patiently for us to come to them, Fred so close to Penny that they were touching.

'Wasn't really our fault, was it Mum?'

'Quiet, son.'

We saw no sign of Lama, and as it was growing late I decided I had to wait until we got back before I searched for her, and search I did when an hour and a half later we returned from the doctor. It was dark. Jeannie, with a bandaged chin and mild concussion, had gone to bed. And for the life of me I could not find Lama.

'Lama! Lama!'

Lama was usually an obedient cat, if it is possible to call any cat obedient. She obeyed because I would choose a moment to call her when I guessed she was in the mood to respond. If my guess was wrong, if my echoing voice reached her while she was on sentry duty beside a tuft of grass or a hole in the hedge, she of course ignored me. Thus her reputation of being obedient depended on me; and a reliable occasion when our minds coincided was at night. She always came home to the comfort of the cottage, to a saucer of milk, to a Jeannie prepared plate of some delicacy, to a deep slumber on our bed. What, then, had happened to her?

I searched the customary hunting grounds, went into the wood flashing my torch, walked round the greenhouses, came back by a bank where for two or three days she had been picking off a family of mice one by one. Then down the track towards the sea, back again to the cottage and up the path to the well. No sign whatsoever, and I began to worry whether Penny in her mad gallop had kicked her; and Lama was lying injured and unable to move. If that were the case she would probably have dragged herself into the undergrowth near by where the accident occurred.

I had now been searching for over an hour, and I wasn't surprised when Jeannie opened a window and called out for news. Nor was I surprised that such was her anxiety she dressed and joined me. Nothing would stop her staying up all night whatever the doctor's orders unless Lama was found.

We had had, of course, these alarms before, and each one had a freshness, an original urgency, a sense that this particular one was at last going to justify our most terrible fears. From a gentle call to a cross one, from a cross call to an anxious one, from an anxious call to loud bleats at the top of our voices: 'Lama! Lama!' And when there was no response, no welcoming small shadow to light up the darkness, we wondered secretly in ourselves in what way the fox had caught her. Had the end been quick or had he carried her away to his earth?

Such foolish fancies vanished like childish nightmares as soon as Lama, having heard us all the time, displaying no remorse, confident of her charms to secure instant forgiveness, suddenly appeared at our feet.

'I've got her!' the favoured one would shout.

The pattern was the same on this occasion. The difference was in the location. The incident of the lane, her flight through the air as Jeannie was falling, her crash among Penny's galloping hooves, had deposited her into a new hunting ground. Never a wanderer far from home, circumstances had forced upon her the opportunity to explore a forbidden land; and when we found her, when my torch shone on her crouching figure, she was awaiting adventure on the edge of a track which Jeannie and I had known since we first came to Minack as a highroad for foxes.

The accident, understandably, had a salutary effect upon us. When next day we held an inquest we admitted we had been growing over-confident, and that the donkeys in future had to be treated with greater respect. We had been behaving towards Penny as if she were an amiable lady without any emotion, and towards Fred as if he were the equivalent of a cuddly puppy. An amateur's attitude. It was high time we imposed discipline upon ourselves in the way we dealt with them.

The first step I took was to ban them from the greenhouse field; and I do not now understand how I had allowed them there in the first place. Four large mobile greenhouses looking like aeroplane hangars were at the mercy of their kicks; and it was a miracle that the only near-damage they ever did was the result of a comical sortie by Fred. One of the mobiles was covering a crop of Christmas lettuce. One day we noticed a series of indentations in the soil and we quickly came to the conclusion that mice had been at work. No plants had been damaged. There were only these holes between the rows.

But Fred was the culprit. He had managed to squeeze through the partly open glass door, and later that day I discovered him making a tour of inspection within. Heaven knows why he did not step on the plants themselves.

The student had left us by the time of this incident and in his place we had a manager; and the object of such a high sounding title was to employ an expert who could steer us away from the confusion in which we were becoming increasingly enmeshed. We had been continuing to lose grip of the flower farm. In the old days when Jane and Shelagh had worked for us, and reliable Geoffrey who had left to go into the building trade, there were no outside commitments to disturb us. We all joined together in the volume of work to do, the slow, meticulous work of a flower farm which has to be done by hand because it cannot be mechanized; and we were, in a sense, all partners. We now looked back with nostalgia to their loyalty and enthusiasm as we struggled to find a way out of our problem. The slow, meticulous work still remained but there was little time to spend on it; and when such work is not regularly and carefully performed, the seasons begin to catch up on each other, crops are planted too late and weeds flourish. I had been seduced from the steady tempo of the past. I was now divided between a life controlled from the city and the life of the peasant which had made Jeannie and me so happy; and what I gained from the one, I lost in the sacrifice of the other. I sat at my desk when my hands should have been in the soil.

We had therefore decided that if we could find a manager, someone so experienced in horticulture that he would demand a high salary, he would take control of the flower farm while I continued with my other work. I would be spared the day-to-day problems and activities but at the same time have the satisfaction of knowing that the flower farm was going to flourish; and of course Jeannie would continue to help with the flowers while I would be there whenever I was needed. In the peak months of the daffodil season, for instance, we would both be happily rushing the flowers away to market as quickly as possible.

I had realized that the type of person we required would be difficult to find. I was warned in fact that the person did not exist; and so I was greatly impressed by the gesture of an applicant who made a special visit from the Channel Islands to see me. He was the only applicant I saw. Because he was so keen to start working at once I engaged him immediately. True enough I was, in any case, in a hurry. The programme of the flower farm had to be kept in motion and there was no time to lose; but I made the error of willing myself to believe he was the man who would suit us, instead of giving time for my head to decide.

He was charming, and had a special wish to live in Cornwall. He won my sympathy because he had been a prisoner of the Japanese. He showed me photographs of his three pretty children. A reference from the market garden where he had been employed for some years was excellent. He liked the cottage I was to rent specially for him. He said he would bring his car over from the Channel Islands and so I took it for granted that he could drive; and of course a driving licence was essential if Jeannie and I were to be spared the time consuming task of driving the Land-Rover whenever a routine journey was necessary. But the day after I had given him his written contract, and I had suggested he collected some things in Penzance, he looked at me with a smile. 'Oh, I don't drive myself,' he said disarmingly, 'my wife does all the driving in our family.'

It was an ominous beginning to our plans for rescuing the flower farm.

XIII

When the foghorns of passing boats hooted in Mount's Bay, the donkeys answered them. They were half believing, I suppose, that somewhere out in the fog were other donkeys. Penny would thrust her head forward and upward and emit the excruciating warble which was her speciality, a wailing saw, a falsetto groan. Fred, still so small that the top of his fluffy back was only just above the level of Penny's rotund belly, followed in a more dignified manner; a real genuine hee-haw, in fact a whole series of hee-haws rising to a crescendo then descending again until it ended quietly in a grunt.

'I laughed out loud alone in my boat,' a fisherman said to me one day, 'listening to your donkeys in the fog yesterday.'

They had, of course, other more subtle forms of communication than their bellows. The snort was a joyous affair much used when they were released in a meadow they hadn't been in for a while; a scamper, a kicking of heels, a friendly dash at each other, heads down and snorts. It was a rich sound. A quick roll of bass drums. A proclamation that they were happy. At other times, I fear, the snort was only a tickle in the nose, grass seeds in a nostril; and then they would stand looking at us by a gate, or peering down at us from the field above the cottage, shaking their heads and snorting, as if they were blaming us for their temporary vexation.

A persuasive, eloquent sound was their whimper. There was nothing obsequious about it. It was a means of making known the fact they had observed us pass by and would appreciate attention or a titbit. They would stand side by side, Penny's white nose topping Fred's white nose, trilling away like birds in a bush; and when we responded, when we advanced towards them speaking words of affection, they changed their whimper into a series of rapid sigh-like sounds. A rush of breath through their nostrils. A curious, puffing method, it seemed, of saying thank you.

They had wonderful eyesight. Sometimes Jeannie and I would go out on a walk to the Carn that we can see from the cottage, a jagged pile of rocks like an ancient castle falling down to the sea. It was a walk on which they generally accompanied us, but as there were succulent grasses all the way on either side of the narrow path, such a walk took a long time. So sometimes we liked to go on our own. Their revenge was to stand in a meadow and watch us, so that when we looked back we could plainly see two re-proachful donkeys, ears pricked, staring in our direction.

'They make me feel awful,' Jeannie would say inevitably, yielding them their victory.

Their eyesight and their acute sense of hearing made them wonderful sentries. Time and again they would warn us by their alertness that a car was coming down the lane long before we heard the tyres on the gravel or that there were voices in the distance. They would point like a game-dog.

'On guard, Jeannie! Look at the donkeys!'

And thereby we had a few minutes grace before the visitor arrived.

One October night, a still, unusually warm night of dense fog, the watchfulness of the donkeys was challenged by an event of great drama. We had left them down in the cliff meadows and this in itself was an adventure for them. They loved these meadows. Not only was there a profusion of their favourite grasses in various stages of growth, but there were also the evergreen privet and escallonia. I had taken them there many times during the daytime but this was the first occasion they had been allowed to stay for the night; and I had done so because when at nightfall I had called them from the gate to come up, they had not taken the slightest notice. They were steep, pocket-sized meadows intertwining one into the other, cascading like stepping stones downwards to the rocks and the sea. Once I used many of them for early potatoes, heaving the sacks up the cliff path; but now they were our daffodil meadows, and in January and February they danced with yellow, the splash of waves on rocks their orchestra. As yet, in October, not even the spikes of green had appeared; and we even, flatteringly, praised the donkeys for being useful. They at least were helping towards keeping the grass trimmed.

I will always wonder whether they were frightened by what happened. Did Fred, more highly strung than Penny, begin immediately to hee-haw? And was he heard by any of the men hanging to the driftwood? It seems certain that he was. And did Penny join in, so that the two of them tolled for the doomed? I can see them in my mind, ears upright like Churchill's victory sign, keen eyes blind in the darkness, noses quivering, listening to the mysterious noises, useless sentinels of disaster.

Jeannie and I were sound asleep with Lama curled at the bottom of the bed. The window was open and as usual, before I went to bed, I had fixed the contraption which we had used ever since, years ago, Monty was nearly caught by a fox as he jumped out of the window on a nightly jaunt. It consisted of wire meshing fitted to a wooden frame the exact size of the window; and so although we could see out and also have the fresh air, Lama was contained in the cottage. It was unsightly but useful; and as soon as we got up it was whisked away.

Anyhow there we were when suddenly I began climbing out of a deep dream, fighting my way reluctantly, until I reached the nightmarish reality of the sound of a car outside the cottage. It was pitch dark, and the car arrived at such speed that when it drew up it woke me by the screech of its brakes. Never before, not even in daylight, had a car arrived so fast. It shot me out of bed. It shot Lama off.

'What's happened?' asked Jeannie dreamily, and in such a tone that I half expected her to tick me off for leaping out of bed and waking her.

'A wreck!' I knew this immediately.

I heard the voices of the men in the first car disappear down the path towards the sea, high chatter folding into silence. Then, as I was struggling into my trousers, another car arrived, then another and another. There were shouts, and orders and counter orders; and when I got outside headlights lit up the grey rocks and the old barn, and pushed their beams at the cottage.

'Here they come,' someone shouted.

There in front of me lurching through the dip of Monty's Leap there came an old jalopy of a van, no, not a van for it had no sides and no ends. Was it a converted hearse? It had a top supported by metal posts at each corner of its chassis, and it carried huge boxes like coffins, and clinging to the sides and heaped on the boxes there seemed to be a legion of swarthy men in woollen skull caps. Heavens, I said to myself, if this weren't the twentieth century these would be pirates. The old jalopy roared up from the Leap, rattling like a hundred clanking tins, a Genevieve of a vehicle, and pulled up inches from a flower bed. The Life Saving team had arrived.

At this moment I smelled the oil.

I wondered why I had not noticed it before as soon as I had woken up. It was not just a whiff of diesel oil. It was as heavy and persistent as night scented stock on a hot summer's night. It filled the air like wood smoke. A ghostly smell, a smell of death, the marker buoy of a wreck. And the reason why I hadn't noticed it before was because, as I learnt later, for over three hours I had been breathing it as I slept, I had become used to it.

It was now half-past six and the fog had gone. A glimmer of light wavered behind the Lizard peninsula and as I looked at it, knowing that within half an hour it would be light and rescue made more simple, a plane roared overhead.

'Where is the wreck?' I asked a man in coastguard's uniform; and as I spoke I thought how absurdly remote I sounded. Here was Minack the hub of the rescue, and I did not belong. I was an onlooker, and I was asking the onlooker's feeble questions.

'We think on the Bucks.'

There was an Inner Buck and an Outer Buck, and in days of sail the scene of many wrecks. They were half a mile off shore from our cliff, small hillocks at low tide, obscured at high tide.

'What kind of boat?'

'Don't know. We've been looking for her since three this morning.'

At a quarter to three Lands End radio had picked up a Mayday signal. It was very feeble and did not last for long. The operator heard enough to learn it was a Spanish ship called the *Juan Ferrer*, but the sender of the signal did not know where he was. He thought, he said, he was near Lands End and he added that the ship was breaking up on the rocks and the captain had ordered her to be abandoned.

Those in charge of the rescue operations were in a quandary. How do we find her? They decided to order the launching of the Sennen lifeboat with instructions she should search the coast between Cape Cornwall and Gwennap Head, the head which is, in fact, the southerly corner of Cornwall, about five miles up the coast from Minack. They also sent out scouts to scour the cliffs, alerted the Mousehole based Penlee lifeboat but did not order her to be launched, and instructed the Life Saving team with their heavy equipment to concentrate in the

Lands End car-park where the headquarters of the rescue operations were set up. For over three hours, therefore, the main rescue services waited patiently in the fog in the car-park, no news from the Sennen lifeboat, no news from the scouts, until at last a report came in that the *Juan Ferrer* was disintegrating on the Bucks.

But the report was wrong. The Life Saving team had already unloaded their equipment from the jalopy and were heaving it down the path, through our big field to the top of the cliff meadows, when one of their number who had gone ahead shouted back that there was no sign whatsoever of a wreck on the Bucks.

The sun behind the Lizard was now brimming over into a canopy of sky, familiar places were becoming recognizable again. I could see the long stretch of sand at Loo Bar, the crinkly cliffs round Mullion, the hills behind Prah Sands pushing like a clenched fist into a low cloud. Closer, I could see again the Carn and the outline of its rocks cascading down to the sea, and the elderberry tree which marked the biggest badger sett in the district. Car lights were switched off. Figures became faces. Torches were put into pockets. Cold realism began taking over from the intangible fantasies of darkness.

A police radio car was now parked opposite the flower house and I could hear distorted voices coming from its loudspeaker. Senior police officers in peaked caps, coastguard officers with weatherbeaten faces, the Life Saving team in their skull caps, all stood around, disconsolate, puzzled, asking themselves over and over again: 'Where's the wreck?'

A field opposite, the one with the gate where the lane turns right for the last hundred yards to Minack, had been turned into a car-park. First one car, then ten, then thirty, their wheels slithering as they turned on the unfamiliar grass. Press photographers and reporters, overdressed for the occasion in neat suits and shiny black shoes, hastened to the cottage. Can we borrow your phone? Sorry, we haven't got one.

And now helicopters from the naval station across the bay at Culdrose began to roar and to hover, up and down the coast. We stood and stared. There in the sky the mid-twentieth century rescue service, here in the shadow of the ancient cottage standing around me the rescue tradition of centuries. 'I dearly love a wreck,' I heard a man say.

At half-past seven someone pointed to a helicopter that was hovering low down off the entrance to Lamorna Cove, a mile or two away, and on the other side of the Carn. 'She's gone in there,' a man said brightly, 'that's what it is. She's gone in the other side of the Carn.'

I felt the sense of relief around me that something positive had been suggested. The men in skull caps lifted their weighty boxes once again and staggered off. A constable went ahead. Pressmen conscientiously set out to wade through the undergrowth. The sun was out, the sea was lazy, shimmering no hint of danger, a robin sang in the wood and a woodpecker laughed, and over everything lingered the smell of oil.

Jeannie suddenly appeared beside me. 'Have you seen the donkeys?' she asked, 'I've been down the cliff and there isn't a sign of them.'

'Oh dear,' I said, 'I'd forgotten about them.'

A policeman on a motor-cycle rode up at that moment, stopped and with measured dignity got off. 'Did you see any donkeys up the lane?' I asked. He looked surprised. 'No sir. I didn't.'

I realized now that they would have been scared out of their wits when the advance party of the Life Saving team dashed down through the meadows, leaving the gate open no doubt for they would hardly have expected to meet donkeys.

'They're probably miles away by now,' I said to Jeannie, and as I spoke I saw in my imagination a bewildered Fred and a distraught Penny plodding along some distant road. 'On the other hand,' I added soothingly, 'They may have only escaped to Pentewan.' These were the neighbouring cliff meadows which we used to rent but gave up after a sequence of gale-ridden crop disasters. 'I'll go and have a look.'

It was past eight o'clock and at the busy centre of Minack there was still no report of the whereabouts of the wreck. Aircraft were zooming overhead and as I made my way over to Pentewan I saw strung along a mile or more offshore a company of ships . . . the Trinity House vessel, the *Stella*, a Dutch tug which was spending the winter in Mount's Bay at a second's readiness to speed for salvage, a Fishery Protection boat and, close to the cliffs as if they were searching the inlets, were the two lifeboats. The Sennen which had been out since the beginning, the Penlee which had been out since half-past six.

I looked over towards the Carn. The group which had set out from Minack were straddled around it. I saw no urgency in their movements. There did not appear to be any reason to believe that they had found the wreck. The only thing which did seem clear to me was that a large number of people other than all of us at Minack must by now know its exact location. The sea was calm, the visibility was excellent, both ships and aircraft must have inspected the length of the coast.

I reached the Pentewan meadows and was passing through what we used to call the thirty lace meadow when I observed piles of driftwood, gulls sweeping and calling above it, drifting eastwards in an endless line towards Lamorna Cove. I had been joined in my walk by a stranger with an important air.

'That settles it,' I said, 'the wreck is the other side of Pentewan cliffs, just beyond the top of that lane we can see. The wreckage is drifting with the tide.'

'The tide has changed,' the man said loftily.

'You mean the wreckage having drifted one way is now

drifting the other?'

'I do.'

I could not contest the views of such a seafaring looking character. It was not my business to inform him that the tide did not change till ten o'clock. But I made up my own mind that the *Juan Ferrer* was on the rocks just over the point ahead.

So it was.

She had rammed the rocks at Boscawen Point within two miles of Minack, a five-hundred-ton cargo boat on passage from Bordeaux to Cardiff with a mixed cargo of onions, plywood made of cedar and thousands of chestnut stakes destined for Welsh farms.

She had gone ashore within four sea miles of the Penlee Lifeboat station; and so if her Mayday signal had been louder, if her position had been able to be plotted, rescuers would have reached her within an hour.

Three survivors jumped ashore. Two men drifted with the tide and the wreckage, and were picked up by the helicopter we saw hovering off Lamorna Cove. Eleven were drowned, their bodies having also drifted with the tide.

And the donkeys? Did they hear the last cries of those men as they drifted past our meadows? And those two who were saved?

It was a special pleasure when all the excitement was over to find they never did run far. While it was still dark and I was dressing, they must have rushed away from the cliff, through the open gate which normally stopped them from cavorting in the garden, into the wood past Boris's house, then on to the farther part of the wood.

When it was all over, when the long adventure ended at nine and we had begun our breakfast, a banshee wail and a tenor-like trumpeting joined in a duet in the corner of the field overlooking the cottage.

Everyone had gone. Minack belonged to its occupants again.

XIV

The *Juan Ferrer* shuddered on the rocks at Boscawen Point for a couple of days, half submerged, disgorging its cargo: and all along the coast men were busy salvaging the stakes and the squares of cedar plywood as they drifted forlornly ashore.

And there were the sightseers. A wreck, like all disasters, has a morbid fascination for those who live safe lives. They heaped themselves on the cliffside, little groups staring in silence, breaking it occasionally to ask the lone policeman, incongruous in helmet, some question he had already answered many times before. Below them, like a whale in its death throes, the object of their entertainment floundered in the waves, sea spouted from the broken windows of the wheelhouse, a rope flopped about the deck, a bell clanged uselessly; and all the while the hulk was heaving this way and that, scraping and banging the rocks, an echoing orchestra of doom, giving a sad, despairing value to the gaping crowd before its inevitable end.

Many of the sightseers came charging along the cliff through Minack meadows to reach their destination. A fanatical lot, a glint in their eyes, walking faster than usual, driving themselves through the undergrowth as if the hounds of hell were after them. 'Where's the wreck?' they panted.

Fred viewed this invasion first with suspicion and then, as the scope of its possibilities dawned upon him, with relish. Here were people galore to show off to. He could divert them from their object, lure from them the praises which would relieve an otherwise dull day. Flattery would be assured. His charm would be irresistible. I am a baby donkey, have you ever seen one before? Look how I can kick my heels and don't you think my fluffy coat adorable? My nose is very soft if you would like to fondle it. Who is the other one? She's my mother. Rather staid. What have you got in that bag?

I might have moved them from the pathway of such attention into the isolation of some other field, but I was in fact delighted there was something to occupy their minds. They were doing no harm, and Fred had a whole series of toys apparently to play with. Each person who passed through was there for his entertainment, and I felt sure he would give value in return.

I was happily believing that this was so when, as I sat at my desk, I saw through the window a hatless elderly man come puffing up the path from the direction of the field, followed a moment later by a formidable looking lady. I dashed out of the cottage to meet them, sensing immediately that something had gone awry.

'Can I help you?' I said, using my usual method of introduction, smiling politely, and at the same time wondering what on earth had happened to cause such obvious excitement.

'Are those your damned donkeys in the field we've just come through?' barked the man. He was out of breath as if he had been running and as he spoke he mopped his bald head with a handkerchief.

'Yes,' I replied doubtfully, 'anything wrong?'

'Very much so,' interrupted the lady grimly looking at me from under an old felt hat, 'the young one snatched my husband's cap and is running round the field with it.'

How had Fred managed it? Had he sneaked up behind the couple as they hurried along, annoyed they had taken no notice of him, and then performed a ballet dancer's leap to take the cap from the gentleman's head?

'Good gracious,' I said, 'I do apologize for this. I'll go ahead straight away and catch him.'

I ran away from them laughing, down the path to the field, asking myself what I would have to do if Fred had gobbled it up. But as I did so I suddenly saw a galloping Fred coming towards me, tweed cap in mouth, and just behind him a thundering, rollicking Penny; and the two of them gave such an impression of joyous, hilarious elation that I only wished that Jeannie had been with me to see them.

The cap was intact, a little wet, but no sign of a tear; and when I thankfully returned it to its owner I asked what had happened. It was simple. It was almost as I imagined it. The couple had sat down on the grass for a rest; and then up behind them came Fred. And away went the cap.

This episode, I am afraid, set the tone of Fred's behaviour towards other sightseers. The trouble, I reckon, was that they were too intent to reach the wreck for them to dally in the way Fred would have liked them to dally. They had no time to play with a donkey. The magnet of disaster destroyed any wish to pause on the way. Morbid curiosity displaced idle pleasure.

Thus, when Fred discovered he was being ignored, he set out to tease. He would watch a group coming along the path from the Carn in the distance, then canter straight at them scattering them in all directions. I found, for instance, three small boys way off the path and waist high in undergrowth, and when I asked how they were there, one of them mournfully replied: 'The donkey chased us, and we're trying to get round.' Of course I then escorted them through the zone of danger and Fred, satisfied with his moral victory, followed meekly behind us until we reached the end of Minack's boundary. Then he scampered back with me, nuzzling me, no longer meek, impatient to play the game again.

He later inveigled me to act as an ally. I began to dislike the ghoulish groups as they strode through Minack private land, not caring about its beauty or that they were there by courtesy, and so I devised a game to play with Fred. He and I would stand in a corner of the field, waiting and watching for a group who looked as if they deserved a surprise. Then, when the chosen victims had reached half-way up the field I would give my order: 'See 'em off, boy!' Away Fred careered, not in an unimaginative dash straight at them, but in a circular movement like a dog rounding up sheep. And after a pause I would hasten after him to reassure our victims that there was nothing really to be scared of in the cavalry charge of a baby donkey.

While the *Juan Ferrer* settled on the bottom of the sea, emotionalism went into action. I have often marvelled how emotionalism, skilfully conducted, can achieve results which the basic facts do not warrant, while other campaigns more worthy but less imaginative in appeal stutter into failure. It is, I suppose, mainly a question of timing. If the perimeter influences are favourable, if the event concerned is sufficiently vivid to act as a flag on a masthead, if worthy people are interested who want an outlet for their energy, if there is a chance for a few to achieve a personal advantage, if all these factors combine to push a cause which appears superficially justified, then the chances are that emotionalism will succeed at the expense of realism.

The object of this particular campaign was to persuade the authorities to build an ocean-type lighthouse a short distance away from Minack in the area Jeannie and I called the Pentewan cliffs. These cliffs and meadows belonged to one of the few remaining unspoilt stretches of the Cornish coast. You could see it from the Carn with the rocks like an ancient castle, and people would stand there and marvel that they could look upon a scene that had been the same since the beginning of time. No man-made ugliness, no breeze block buildings to offend them.

'Every day of our lives,' I wrote in *A Drake At The Door*, 'was spent in unison with this coast, the rage of the gales, salt smearing our faces as we walked, east winds, south winds, calm summer early mornings, the first cubs, a badger in the moonlight, wild violets, the glory of the first daffodil, the blustering madness of making a living on land that faced the roar of the ages.

'The cliffs fall to rocks black and grey where the sea ceaselessly churns, splashing its foam, clutching a rock then releasing it, smothering it suddenly in bad temper, caressing it, slapping it as if in play, sometimes kind with the sun shining on the white ribbon of a wave, a laughing sea throwing spray like confetti, sometimes grey and sullen, then suddenly a sea of ungovernable fury lashing the cliffs; enraged that for ever and for ever the cliffs look down.

'And among the rocks are the pools; some that tempt yet are vicious, beckoning innocently then in a flash a cauldron of currents, pools that are shallow so that the minnow fish ripple the surface as they dash from view, pools so deep that the seaweed looks like a forest far below, inaccessible pools, pools which hide from everyone except those who belong to them.

'High above, the little meadows dodge the boulders, and where the land is too rough for cultivation the bracken, the hawthorn, the brambles, the gorse which sparks its yellow the year round, reign supreme. This is no place for interlopers. The walkers tamed by pavements, faced by the struggling undergrowth, turn back or become angry, their standardized minds piqued that they have to trace a way through; and it is left to the few, the odd man or woman, to marvel that there is a corner of England still free from the dead hand of the busybody.

'Here, on our stretch of the coast, man has not yet brought his conceit.'

For some years there had been murmurs about erecting a small, harbour-type light and fog signal near Lamorna Cove to act like a street lamp for the benefit of local fishermen on their way to and fro from Mousehole or Newlyn;

and this indeed was a reasonable proposition. But the wreck of the *Juan Ferrer* gave a new twist to this idea, and the cry went up for an ocean-type lighthouse, as powerful as that on the Wolf Rock and the Lizard; and the cries became louder after a television film was compiled called Cornish Wrecks. It was a stirring production and somehow succeeded in giving the impression that there had been twenty-three wrecks in twelve years on this southern coast of the Lands End peninsula which the new lighthouse would serve. Almost two wrecks a year within a distance of ten miles! The film caused a furore.

This was wonderful material for the campaigners and I watched with fascination how they reacted. Women's organizations were roped in. A petition was organized and signatures were collected by door-to-door canvassers. A letter was sent to Sir Winston Churchill. A question was asked in the House of Commons. A special programme of the T.V. film was shown to Mr Marples as the man finally responsible for instructing Trinity House to build the lighthouse. Veiled accusations were made that Trinity House should have acted before. The Minister must act! Gradually, with the persistence of a steamroller, the illusion was fostered and believed that a new lighthouse would banish wrecks from the Cornish coast for ever.

The snag of the illusion lay in the facts which the campaigners seemed to avoid. There had not been twenty-three wrecks in twelve years; there had been four wrecks in over fifteen years. And there were other facts which the campaigners ignored with aplomb as they hurried on their emotional way. Another four wrecks, in as many years, had occured within a few hundred yards of lighthouses; two off the Longships near Lands End, two at Pendeen near Cape Cornwall. Seventeen had died in one of them the year before.

The claim, therefore, that lighthouses provided immunity to those who sailed in their neighbourhood was unfortunately untrue; twentieth-century methods of safe-guarding shipping were required, not those of the seven-teenth. Moreover, in the case of the new lighthouse, it was to be situated at a position which many experienced sailors found incomprehensible. Tater-du, as the position is called, is five miles from the headland called Gwennap Head marking the southernmost point of the Lands End penin-sula; five miles, in fact, inside Mounts Bay. 'If they want one at all,' said an old fisherman to me who had sailed this coast all his life, 'put it on Gwennap Head or close to it. There it might help shipping coming up the Channel or across from the Lizard. But it's crazy to put it so far inside the Bay as Tater-du for a score of reasons.'

The campaigners swept forward, irresistible, vociferous, unreal in their arguments, thriving on the unproven slogan they were saving lives; and there is today a lighthouse at Tater-du. In this age of electronics, of radio direction find-ing and radar, a lighthouse of hideous utility design with huge electricity pylons marching across the skyline towards it, the first to be built in this country since the last century, costing many thousands of pounds, now climbs into the sky, a phalanx of concrete blocks, on this lovely once lonely coast.

A monument to what happens when emotionalism goes into action.

XV

Fred met his first winter and viewed it with apprehension. No one to visit him. No flavour in the grass. Hedgerows bare. Long nights with nothing to do. Driving rain to flatten his fluffy coat. And gales.

How he hated gales. Rain, however heavy, was only an inconvenience in comparison. He would stand in the rain hour after hour, spurning the welcoming open door of the stables, looking miserable nevertheless, taking apparently some kind of masochistic pleasure out of his discomfort. I was sorry for him in the rain but I did not feel I was under any obligation to take steps to protect him from it. A really persistent long day's rain would put him in a stupor, and if I called him he would pause a moment or two before lifting his head dazedly to look at me. He seldom showed any wish to come to me; he and Penny, heads down, the rain dripping of their noses, bottoms towards the weather, would stand stoically content in what I would have thought were intolerable conditions.

But in gales he needed protection. He became restless as soon as the first breeze, the scout of the gale, began hurrying across the field; and he would begin to hee-haw, lifting his head to the scurrying clouds so that a mournful bellow joined the swish of the wind in the trees. He would not stand still, racing round in small circles, then dashing off to another part of the field; and instead of following Penny dutifully about as was his usual custom, Penny would be hastening after him. He was the leader. It was as if he believed that something tangible was chasing him, not a gale but an enemy with plans to capture him. A foolish fantasy of the very young, faced by the unknown.

Penny herself, with private memories of the Connemara mountains, was unperturbed. She felt, no doubt, that Fred's fears were part of his education, and that repetition would dull them. She plodded after him as he ran hither and thither like an old nanny after a child, and when he grew tired she nudged him along to the shelter of a hedge. Penny was very weather-wise. She had mapped each meadow with a number of tactical positions to suit every variation of the wind; a series of well worn patches on the ground disclosed them. Thus, if a westerly moved a few points to the east resulting in her current position being exposed, she cunningly led the way to the next patch.

But there were times when the gales roared like a squadron of supersonic hedgehopping aircraft, deafening us in the cottage so that when the news came on I had to switch the radio at full stregth if we were to hear the announcer. Lama would be curled up comfortably in a chair, Boris in his house in the wood would be sitting on his perch; the gulls, Knocker and Squeaker or the lonely, friendly Peter, would be safe beneath some leeward cliff until many hours later the gale died down and they set off to fly to the roof again.

It was at a time like this that I indulged in protecting Fred. At first I used to lead the two of them to the shelter of the wood, and they would stand around the outside of Boris's house among the ivy covered trunks of the elms, the wind slapping the tops, swaying, branches cracking and falling, an invisible angry hate hissing its fury, mad with rage that its omnipotent, conquering, horizon-leaping triumph over the sea was being checked by hands held high; trees and hills and houses and sudden valleys, old buildings and church spires, hedges acting as ramparts. Penny and Fred would stand there with the roar of the gale above them and the roar of the sea behind them. They did not like it.

And so in due course, whenever a gale blew, I took them

to the stable meadow where the security of the stable awaited them. In a severe gale you would find both of them within. In any kind of wind you would always find Fred.

The stable was dilapidated but solid. It was an ancient building with arm-length thick walls made of stone in all shapes and sizes and bound together by clay. The clay in many places outside had cracked and fallen away over the years, and sparrows and blue tits made use of the holes in the spring; one wall was so popular with the sparrows that their nests resembled a series of flats, each one above the other. Huge beams stretched across the battered ceiling inside, rusty hooks where once hung harness stared from the walls, cobble stones like knuckles of a hand lined the floor, and in the corner there was the broken frame of a manger.

On Christmas Eve we took mince pies to the donkeys in the stable. A lighthearted gesture, a game for ourselves, an original diet for them.

'Donkeys! Donkeys!' Jeannie called into the darkness of the meadow, 'come into the stables. We've got something for you.' And after a minute or two, their shadows loomed, heralded by inquiring whimpers.

'Fred,' I said, 'you're about to have your first mince pie.'

Inside we lit a candle in an old-fashioned candlestick and put it on the window sill. The light flickered softly. It flickered on their white noses, their eager faces, their giant rabbit-like ears. They pushed their heads forward, nuzzling us in expectation.

'Patience, patience!' said Jeannie, holding the mince pies high in her hand, 'don't be in such a hurry!' And then with a quick movement she gave one to each of them.

As I stood there watching I began to feel the magic of the occasion. Our intention had been to have a joke, to enjoy the merry spirit of Christmas and now, unexpectedly, something else was taking place.

'Look at their crosses,' I said to Jeannie. The cross of Penny was black merging into black, but that of Fred was easy to see; the dark line tracing up the backbone beneath his fluffy brown coat until it reached his shoulders, then stopping abruptly when it met the two lines tracing down each foreleg. 'Here we are,' I went on, 'with two biblical creatures eating mince pies.'

'In a stable.'

'On Christmas Eve.'

There was the gentle sound as they shifted their feet on the cobblestones, and I was aware too of the musty scent of their coats. Ageless simplicity, laughed at, beaten, obstinately maintaining an individuality; here indeed was a moment when there was a communication with the past. Struggle, self sacrifice, integrity, loyalty; how was it that the basic virtues, the proven talisman of man's true happiness, was being lost in the rush of material progress? Why was it that civilization was allowing its soul to be destroyed by brain power and the vacuous desire it breeds? Why deify the automaton when selflessness has to be won? For a shimmering moment we felt the race halted. No contrived, second-hand emotion. We were not watching, we were part. As it always had been, so it was now.

We had changed since we had first known each other, Jeannie and I. Once we had both fought hard to savour flattery and power, to be part of a glad world of revelry, to be in the fashion, and to rush every day at such speed that we disallowed ourselves any opportunity to ponder where we were going; and now we were in the stable at a customary moment of merriment, perfectly happy, alone with two donkeys. It is easy to remain in a groove, a groove which becomes worn without you realizing it, only recognizable by friends who have not seen you for a long time, and it is usually luck which enables you to escape. Jeannie and I had the luck to feel the same at the same time, and so we had been united in forcing ourselves to flee our conventional background. There had never been any argument between us about the pros and cons, gradually the standards we once believed so important appeared sadly ineffectual, only vital until they had been experienced. Moreover the merciless zest required to achieve them became an exhausting effort as soon as the standards, reached at last, had to be maintained; for it became obvious to us that in most cases the banners of success were made of paper, waved by *entrepreneurs* who were temporarily leeching on the creative efforts of others.

Thus Jeannie and I belonged to the lucky ones who, having seen their personal horizon, had also reached it; and yet in doing so there was no possible reason for self satisfaction. It was true that contentment was always near us, but there was an edge to our life which stopped us from ever taking it for granted. What had become our strength was the base to which we could retreat. We had a home we loved. Around us was the ambience of permanency. We had roots. And so, when we became involved in sophisticated stresses which touched us with memories of other days, there was a moat behind which we could recharge. We then could observe quietly the enemy; envy, for instance, the most corroding of sins, the game of intrigue which fills so many people's lives, the use of the lie which in business is considered a justifiable weapon, the hurt that comes from insecurity, the greed which feeds on itself, the worship of headline power without quality to achieve it. We watched, and sometimes we were vexed, sometimes we were frightened. Across the moat we could see the reflection of the past.

On occasions we were interviewed for magazines, radio and television, and Jeannie usually had to take the brunt of the questions. And how weary she grew of that inevitable question: 'Don't you miss all the gay times you had at the Savoy?' She would smile brightly and say no, and there would follow the second stock question. 'Don't you ever say to yourself that you would like to go back?' These leading questions demanded an affirmative answer, or at least a hesitation on Jeannie's part. Instead the second no was as firm as the first. Jeannie always failed to gratify any outsider's hope that she might be dissatisfied in a life so different from that she described in *Meet Me At The Savoy*.

One day a distinguished interviewer arrived with a caravanserai of cameramen and others at half-past eight in the morning at Minack. Dapper and trim in a city suit and shiny black shoes, looking like a stockbroker on the way to the office, he stepped up the path and into the cottage. He left over twelve hours later. An illuminating day.

The tone was set by a tough, preliminary cross-examination, as if Jeannie and I were suspected partners in crime; and in the best tradition of detection, we were questioned separately. First myself, then Jeannie; and when we compared notes afterwards we found we had each endured a similar, attacking interrogation the aim of which was to discover the weakness in our happiness. '*What* do you quarrel about?' was the first question he put to Jeannie.

But as the day wore on, we became aware once again of the loneliness which besets an idol whom everyone admires but few have time to know. He did not wish to hurt us. His screen self was confused with his true self. He had to maintain his image and so he was trying to knock us down. Perhaps he saw in us what he wanted for himself, a happy marriage and the time to enjoy it; and thus he hoped to explode our way of life in order to reassure himself that conventional happiness was impossible. He wanted reality but was trapped by outward success; he had to live with the bathroom door open or the public would rage. I found it strange to watch him straddled in an armchair at the end of the day, staring gloomily into the fire, whisky glass in hand, and to know that he represented in the eyes of millions their imaginary ideal of twentieth-century contentment, a conqueror of the small screen. All I saw myself was a man who spent his life shuffling from one arc lamp to another, secretly cherishing a hope that a home one day awaited him.

Jeannie and I had the home but we were, on the other hand, disorganized. I sometimes felt I behaved like a rabbit caught in the glare of headlights dashing this way and that without purpose until it zigzags its way to the safety of a burrow. I seemed incapable of solving the problems around me. I would have one idea, then another, then another, and none of them would ever quite come off. I was safe at Minack but I was not progressing. My imagination became congealed, for instance, by the tedious detail of spending three days, Jeannie beside me, on my hands and knees weeding freesias; and we would both become doped by the simplicity of the task. We would cheer when we had finished. We would gaze in admiration at the neat beds and convince ourselves that something worthwhile had been achieved. So it had been. Unhappily it was at the price of thinking. There is a soothing, narcotic daziness in weeding which pleasingly seduces you from concentrating on plans for the future. A day of weeding might satisfy our consciences but it did not advance us. It only helped to obscure the trouble we were in.

The manager remained charming and anxious to please. He laughed often and apologized handsomely whenever it was necessary, but as we shivered slowly towards the daffodil season, it was clear he was not the man we had been looking for. Able in many horticultural departments, always pleasant and amiably tempered, it was no fault of his good nature that he did not unfortunately fit into our type of flower farm. Thus Jeannie and I were now in a web of our own making, and our position was far more difficult than before he arrived.

We were, for instance, embroiled in the man's life. We were not a large soulless organization which could upturn the life of an individual 'for the good of the Company'. His three children were now at local schools. There were no other jobs in the district which would suit his managerial manner. Thus if he left us the children's schooling would be disrupted when they were just growing accustomed to their new surroundings. The family had no permanent home. The cottage we rented for them was their home until they could find somewhere else to go.

'We'll have to compromise,' I said at last.

'How?'

'The best thing we can do is to concentrate on the next three months, keep him for that time, and let the summer look after itself.'

It was the only thing we could do. The daffodil season was advancing upon us with the massive inevitability of a steam roller. There would be three hundred thousand individual blooms to pick, bunch, pack and send away to Covent Garden. Every day would be a race against time, against the lowering of prices, against the gales which always threatened; the blooms were never secure from being destroyed in the meadows until they rimmed the pails in the packing shed. And I was still writing *A Drake At The Door*. I could not break away and put my full mind to the flower farm. All I could do was to shut my eyes to the future, and aim to salvage what we could from the huge harvest of daffodils. I had no time in which to attempt a reorganization. I had to muddle through; and when it was all over, and we were in a vacuum, we would then pause and ponder which way we had better go.

We would then decide whether to continue with the flower farm or to give it up.

XVI

When the snow came after Christmas we shut the donkeys in the stable at night. We did it for our own peace of mind. We could not bear to lie in bed and think of them out there in the dark becoming snow donkeys; and yet, as experience proved, they did not seem to object. One evening when we returned home late and snow was falling, we found the two foolish things out in the meadow despite the fact the comfort of the stable awaited them.

Fred was like a small boy in the snow. The first morning he was introduced to it, he came rushing out of the stable, stopped in his tracks when he saw it, began pawing with his front feet, put his head down and pushed his nose into it, then in wild excitement started a fandango of flying kicks which made me speedily run away from him. Then he raced into the middle of the meadow and without more ado sank to his knees which was, of course, the preliminary to a roll.

The roll, in normal circumstances, was a solemn ritual. The ceremony was performed on a small circular patch in a carefully chosen position and, as it was well worn, the ground was either dusty or muddy according to the weather. This, however, had no bearing on the success of the ceremony, for the roll was a donkey bath; and whether Fred rose from his roll in a cloud of dust or caked in mud, he was satisfied. As far as he was concerned he was clean. He had had his wash.

Penny, like a fat lady on the seashore, had to watch her dignity when she followed suit. She would collapse to her knees, fall over to one side, then begin to wriggle this way and that in an endeavour to complete a roll. It was an embarrassing sight. She would get on her back, a huge grey barrel facing up to the heavens, then miserably fail to force herself over. Nor would her attempts be silent. She, like Fred, accompanied her efforts with repetitive, body-shaking grunts. A desperate sound, like a wrestler in combat; and when, if we were watching, she at last succeeded in making it by a final glorious lurch, Jeannie and I would send up a cheer. She would then get up, turn her back on us, stare at an imaginary interest in the distance, and pretend that nothing whatsoever untoward had happend.

Fred's roll in the snow, however, was purely a gesture of joy. He was captivated by the feeling of the powdery stuff, and he rolled this way and that snorting with pleasure, kicking his heels in the air, and when he had had enough and stood up again, he looked as if he were a donkey wrapped in cotton wool. He then hoped for a game. Ears pinned back, head on one side, one could sense he was laughing at the huge joke of it all; and when I began gently throwing snowballs at him, I was surprised he did not pick one up himself and chuck it back. He wanted to, I'm sure.

We had no fear that the bitter weather might affect our daffodils. It delayed them, of course, and for weeks they stayed constant a few inches above the ground, too cold to move; and instead of starting to harvest them in the middle of January, we had to wait until the middle of February. Our main concern centred round the freesias, for their peak flowering time coincided with the day and night frost. It was awful. We had a splendid crop but our heaters did not have the power to lift the temperature sufficiently, and although they kept the frost out they did not make the air warm enough to bring the buds into bloom. The heaters, using huge amounts of oil, curled the equivalent of pound notes into the chill air; but the plants did not move, and because of this the roots began to develop a disease. Then, when one week we picked enough to send a consignment to

Covent Garden, they froze on the way. The van was un-heated, and the consignment was unsaleable.

The donkeys, meanwhile, were becoming restless. There was nothing for them to nibble, and we fed them on pel-lets, hay and anything they might fancy. It was one long round of eating, and as the ground was too hard for any serious exercise, they began to store up energy; and the energy unleashed itself as soon as the soft winds began to blow again and the frost disappeared. And then twice they disappeared.

At other times of the year we would have been annoyed, but not worried. But on these occasions their disappear-ance coincided not only with the time the daffodils were coming into bloom; it was also potato planting time. Neither among the daffodils nor on the newly-turned soil could donkey feet be anything else but a trouble maker.

I had already suspected that some of our neighbours might have considered the donkeys as parasites. After all we had been asked any number of times during the summer by visitors, 'Don't they *do* anything?' And if the visitors asked such questions it was understandable that farmers might be asking them too. They could see them meandering aimlessly around the meadows, creatures that wouldn't draw carts, couldn't be milked, and incapable of performing any farming activity. Nor were they proving the success at keeping the grass down that I had hoped. They were choosey. They would eat certain grasses and certain weeds, but I was astonished how much was always left behind; and a meadow had still to be cut down after their presence had been intended to clear it. We felt they *ought* to do something, and so when the daffodil season began we got hold of two Spanish onion baskets. We tied them together and put the rope across Penny's back so the baskets rested against either flank, then we led her to a daffodil meadow and filled the baskets with the stems we picked. It was a total failure. For one thing it was obviously much simpler and quicker to fill an ordinary hand basket, then put it in the back of the Land-Rover; for another, Fred, who was too young to be asked to share in the task, treated the whole effort as a game. He butted the baskets with his head. He whinnied. He was, in fact, a nuisance.

I could not, therefore, tell anyone that they performed any useful function, but it was easy to answer the other regular question: 'What do you have them for?' I explained they gave pleasure both to ourselves and to strangers, and that they were plainly happy in themselves. Every day they were becoming more affectionate and more trusting; and the responsibility of looking after them, which once I had feared, had turned instead into a reward. They enriched the tapestry of our life at Minack; and by touching us with their mystical quality of antiquity provided a reminder that in an age when the machine is king, all life is still sacred whether it has wings, or two legs, or four. There was another, more personal feature about them which perhaps only Jeannie and I could understand. They had become to us a symbol. They were the tangible reflection of the simple life which we were struggling to maintain in the face of the outside stresses which were trying to envelop us.

Such thoughts, however, would not excuse damage to the crops of my neighbours, and the first time they disappeared I got into a panic when a passing hiker told me he had seen two galloping donkeys half a mile away over the opposite hill. There was, I knew, a field of broccoli in that direction, and another field of freshly planted potatoes; and I saw in my mind an enraged farmer striding towards me. And so Jeannie and I set off at the double, halters in our hands, praying silently that no neighbour would see us and that the capture would be quickly achieved nd that no damage had been done in the meantime. Ten minutes later we arrived panting at the open gate of a grass field, and in the far corner stood the donkeys. Even from that distance they gave the impression of solemnity. They were in a fix, they were far from home, and they were wishing they had never started on their escapade; and so when Jeannie called out, 'Donkeys! Donkeys!' they turned their heads in our direction, then meekly, thankfully trotted towards us.

They disappeared for a second time three days later and the panic was repeated because the direction we guessed they had taken was towards Jack Cochram's cliff potato meadows. He and Walter Grose had just completed the laborious task of planting them by shovel, the centuries-old method which could not be improved upon because no machine would work the small meadows which fell like stepping stones to the sea. And I knew that if the donkeys began prancing over the newly-turned earth, real damage would be done. Their hooves would crush the seed potatoes which were only a few inches beneath the surface.

So once again Jeannie and I rushed off with the halters, this time with a certain impatience. We had thought the previous excursion had taught them a lesson, that they were ashamed of themselves, and that they would cling to Minack land in the future; and we were in part correct in our assumption. We did not find them among Jack and Walter's cliff meadows. We found them among ours. I had left the gate open at the top of our cliff and I found them at the bottom, roaming contentedly in a splendid meadow of Magnificence daffodils which were waiting to be picked.

They did not escape again. Instead, as the daffodil season increased its speed, leaving us no time to dally with them, they would stand and reproachfully stare at us. They could not understand why we were rushing about so fast. Neither did the gulls who cried from the roof for their bread, nor Boris who flapped his big wings in impatience as he waited at the door for his scraps. This was the time when every minute means money, and we could not break away from our routine to pander to them. Only Lama remained serene. She pottered about catching mice in the grass and the hedges, resting herself in the lane after a capture, silky black against grey chippings, paying us a call in the packing shed, jumping up on a bench, purring for a while among the daffodil pails, then off again on her business. She was as tired as we were when the day was ended.

We began the season by bunching the daffodils in bud, the new method of bunching which means the daffodils last far longer after they have been bought in the shop. Formerly the markets insisted on the blooms being full out when they arrived in their boxes, and inevitably this usually meant that they were a few days old when they reached the customer. The new method is also far more convenient for the daffodil grower because he can pick the buds, put the stems in water for a couple of hours, then pack them and send them away the same day. Previously the daffodils had to linger in pails perhaps for two or three days before they were ready for market; and this resulted in valuable space being taken up in the packing shed. Buds, therefore, are an excellent idea both for grower and customer despite the fact they may not appear so attractive to buy. Unfortunately on this particular occasion in this particular season, Jeannie and I were faced with a snag. We could not pick the daffodils fast enough to stop them coming full out naturally in the meadows.

It was a sweet spring. No gales seemed to threaten us, and following the bitter winter the various varieties leapt forward together as soon as the earth was warmed. It was a bumper crop, every bulb burst into bloom instead of the customary misses, and Minack meadows were covered with potential income. And when these meadows are yellow against the backdrop of a deep blue sea even the cynic will marvel, even the man whose salary is derived from destroying by words or by vision, even the devil would not deny it is one of the most beautiful sights in the world.

My first job in the morning was to drain the pails of water so that the daffodils we had bunched the previous day had time to dry before Jeannie began packing them. She was a deft packer. I would help her by getting the boxes ready, cardboard type boxes which arrived from the suppliers in large flat bundles, and I had to fold each one into shape; and into the boxes Jeannie would pack sometimes twelve bunches, sometimes fifteen, sometimes eighteen, depending upon the variety. Then I would tie the boxes in couples, label them, stack them in the Land-Rover, and rush off to Penzance station to catch the flower train.

All day we would bunch. It is one of the most soothing tasks you could wish for, and as each bunch is completed and you hold it up and look at it to make quite sure that each bloom is perfect, you experience the naïve pleasure that within forty-eight hours it will be lighting up a room; and you feel you are lucky indeed to be performing a task which earns such a reward.

And while we bunched, the manager was conscientiously picking in the meadows. He would fill the baskets, carry them to the Land-Rover which I would leave in some convenient place, then report to me that all the baskets were full; and then, because he could not drive, I left my bunching and drove the Land-Rover back to the packing shed.

After he had gone home for the day, Jeannie and I would go out together to pick and as, bent double, we went up and down between the beds we would call out to each other inconsequential remarks.

'Strange how the Mags never flower as well as California.'

'Do you remember Jane in this meadow shaking a shovel above her head at an aeroplane because she'd read in the paper it was testing West Cornwall for uranium?'

'And it was over there behind those elders that Shelagh hid to watch the cubs play.'

'This basket is too heavy for me. Could you get me

another one?'

'Here comes the *Scillonian*. She's done an extra trip today so that means the market will be flooded tomorrow.'

'Damn, I've pricked my finger on a bracken stump.'

'Look at this lovely rogue! What daffodil can it be?'

'Silly name, rogue. Who gave it I wonder? And yet it' graphic. A daffodil which doesn't belong to the variety which one is picking.'

'I wish Geoffrey was with us. We would have finished picking this meadow ages ago. The fastest picker I've ever known. I bet he'd prefer doing this to driving a lorry for a builder.'

'I wonder if he would.'

The shadows fall early on our cliff. The setting sun is still comparatively high behind the hill when the rocks begin to point their fingers towards the sea. It becomes cool when on the top of the hill it is still warm. You soon have a sense of impending sleep, a settling for the night as the confetti of gulls drift against the dying sky, floating to smooth rocks, calling from time to time. I would then carry the baskets we had filled up the steep path to the field, load them into the Land-Rover, and the two of us would drive up the field and along the track to Minack. The same track, the same view awaiting us, as when years before, at a moment of despair, we looked ahead of us, and Jeannie called out as our problems had been solved: 'Look! There's a gull on the roof!'

XVII

The daffodil season was over, and we were once again sitting on the white seat beside the bare verbena bush having our breakfast. Like the wink of an eyelid the year had gone.

The familiar beds of green foliage, spattered by occasional left-over blooms, stretched side by side in the meadows of the cliff. Wasted flowers straddled the compost heap outside the packing shed. And in the shed itself there was the usual collection of cardboard flower boxes, half-torn pieces of packing paper, a ball of string with a pair of scissors across the top of it, three bunching cradles, galvanized pails on the shelves, the odd crushed stem on the floor, invoice books and contents labels lying on the table, all waiting for the spring clean we would be giving the packing shed as soon as we had had a pause.

'Well, the season's over,' I said, watching Boris waddling towards us, 'and I'm sorry.'

'Me too.'

'Now we have to face facts.'

Lama was stalking past Boris. His friendliness towards her was often tinged with jealousy. He was now hissing away at her like an old steam engine, stretching out his neck and beak as if he would dearly like to take a bite out of her tail. She was, as usual, beatific in her indifference. She was immune from danger. She had a great love for everyone and everything around Minack, so why should he worry? She was not jealous of Boris. Her life was too idyllic for mean thoughts.

'I told the man,' I went on, breakfast over and fumbling for my pipe, 'that his family can stay on in the cottage until the school term ends in July.'

'I can't see what else we could have done,' said Jeannie, making a grab for Lama as she passed by but missing her, 'but without a cottage we haven't got a hope of replacing him.'

At this moment a tremulous hoot, rapidly changing into a hiccuping, roaring bray echoed from the field above the cottage. A calculated thought behind the noise. A cunning knowledge of the power of such blackmail. A certainty that the summons would be answered.

'Fred,' I said solemnly, 'is requiring attention.' And we got up from the seat to go and talk to him.

Our problem had the same common denominator of all people who work on their own. When everything goes smoothly one can rejoice that one is not answerable to any boss. One is independent in a regimented world, and one is inclined to believe that one is also independent of trouble. Unfortunately trouble when it comes is magnified; and a problem is more difficult to solve because there are no reserves to draw upon.

In our case there was the inescapable fact that without reliable help I could not work the flower farm and at the same time cope with the sophisticated, other side of our life. There was so much heavy work to be done, tractor driving and ploughing, keeping the meadows in trim, all the slogging work of a skilled labourer. I had done all this in other years, and would have done it again if there had been time, but now there was no time. I had legions of letters to answer, people endlessly calling to see us, and there were too the painful, slow hours of writing. I had gained so much, but I had lost much too. And amidst all the kindness that Jeannie and I were receiving, there were signs of the same jarring influences which we had disliked so much before we came to Minack. The standards of the competitors in the rat race seemed more offensive than ever.

Fred was in a thoughtful mood when we reached him. He stood on the edge of the field staring down into the small garden, a gentle, harmless little donkey who could not possibly have been responsible for the appalling noise of a few minutes before. Penny was a few yards away up the slope of the field, silhouetted against the sky and looking alertly in our direction, her coat now glistening black, her splendid head etched like a thoroughbred. Then, not wishing to miss any gifts which might be available, she trundled towards us. They stood together, nose beside nose.

'Here you are both of you,' said Jeannie, and she gave them each a jam tart, 'you can't have any more because these are the last in the tin.'

They ate the tarts, waited hopefully for more, then ambled away together into the field. We paused for a moment watching them, the blue sky as a backdrop, first nuzzling each other, then breaking away and racing each other at the gallop to the far end where the wood joins the field. Jeannie suddenly said: 'I've got a wonderful idea. The donkeys have given me it!'

'Well?'

'A year ago we were about to have a holiday when Penny's arrival stopped it.'

'Needless to say I haven't forgotten.'

'We can't possibly think of going away in the foreseeable future because there is no one to look after the animals.'

'Agreed.'

'So why don't we behave like the donkeys . . . and be idle?'

I put my arm round her shoulders. I was laughing. 'Such a suggestion,' I said, 'is amoral.'

'We would be holiday makers,' she said, ignoring me, 'like all those people who come to see us.'

'And close our eyes to crops, weeds and the existence of greenhouses?'

'Yes . . . and stop worrying about labour problems!'

'You're persuading me, Jeannie.'

'We would have the time to watch the summer peacefully instead of fighting against it.'

'Just laze on the rocks.'

'And fish. I've always wanted a fishing rod.'

'I can't see you taking the fish off the hook once you've caught it.'

'I'd have the leisure to work on the garden and experiment with all sorts of recipes.'

'You're making my mouth water.'

'Don't laugh at me.'

'I'm not. I am thinking how strange it is that you should lead me astray.'

'That's not true. A time comes for everyone when they need a pause. And that's what I'm suggesting.'

'Isn't this a surrender?'

'Of course not, you idiot. I'm only saying that instead of struggling with the impossible we should have an interval.'

'And be Micawbers during the course of it.'

'Yes.'

'All right,' I said, 'you've convinced me. When shall we start this idleness?'

'Why not this morning?'

I was laughing again. 'If that's the case the donkeys deserve a reward. I'll fetch them an apple each.'

For a month we were as gay as could be. Jeannie had her fishing rod, dangled a line for hours into our teaspoon of a bay, and caught nothing. I pottered about, leant against rocks staring vacantly out to sea, pretending there never would be worries again. People called and instead of being as polite as was necessary before brushing them away, we indulged in their company. There was no cause for impatience. There was no tedious task niggling our minds, no weeding, no sense of duty to make us feel we were wasting time by talk. We were relaxed. We behaved as I would have expected two people to behave who had rented Minack for a holiday.

But when the month had gone, there slowly began to build up an unexpected dimension in our lives. Our consciences started to prick. We found, for instance, that a green-house which is left empty when by natural right it should be occupied develops an air of resentment; and we had six greenhouses. They stared at us day after day, huge canopies of glass, and although we tried to keep our eyes averted as we passed them, they forced us to look; and we shuddered increasingly at the sight of the weeds growing with lush abandon. At the end of the month the contents resembled a section of the South American jungle.

A further discomfiture was not only did we feel guilty, but we were publicly proved guilty. When callers arrived we of course could not prevent them from observing what was happening, or coming to their own conclusions; and so we imagined their eyes became shifty, as if they believed they had discovered the skeleton in our cupboard; and that we were now playing at flower farming because we had been seduced by the shadowy rewards from the city. We became increasingly uncomfortable. We shuddered in guilty anticipation as soon as we saw a car coming down the lane. And every day the weeds prospered abundantly.

Callers reserved their comments until they had left us. Friends didn't. Sage advice has often been heaped upon us by friends enjoying a Cornish holiday. Normally the safety of an office protects one from the amateur, but in our case the office was there for all to see. Everyone could participate. And often we have been maddeningly irritated when friends, having absorbed our time, have innocently commented on some feature of the flower farm with which, in any case, we ourselves were dissatisfied. A question of rubbing salt in a wound.

This time, however, our friends were blunt. And in the wake of their remarks, however unreasonable they may have been, we found ourselves wallowing in wordy explanations.

'It is beyond me why you've left these greenhouses empty. They look a mess.'

'What is in that meadow over there, the one with all the nettles in it?'

'Surely you could find time to grow cucumbers. My aunt grows them and finds them very easy.'

'I hope you realize that these greenhouses are depreciating all the time, and you're not getting a penny interest on your capital.'

In other years we would have loftily dismissed these strictures as an unasked-for interference, grumbled together privately, then forgotten them. This summer, however, with our consciences pricking, we were peculiarly sensitive to criticism and so sometimes we accompanied our wordy explanations with a dash of bad temper. The truth is that the honeymoon of doing nothing about the flower farm was soon over. Worry took its place again.

I am among those who can be down in the depths one moment and up in the heights the next. I also wilt, my imagination becomes stifled, when faced by people who show no likelihood of ever sharing my wavelength; and the fact they so obviously believe in their superiority over me only increases my frustrated fury. But I take wings when I meet someone who possesses the gift of enthusiasm and who distributes it among those with whom he has dealings. My mind awakes. I am willing to climb Everest.

One hot afternoon we had a caller who was the salesman for our flowers in Covent Garden. Of all the business people I have ever met, flower salesmen are the most genial, despite the early morning hours they have to keep, and the dark, cold conditions of the market in which they work; and for the 10 per cent they receive from sales, they also give the grower much enthusiasm and very helpful advice, This, at any rate, is what Jeannie and I have found over the years in sending all our flowers to the same firm in

Covent Garden. Moreover, they took such a personal interest in the flowers they received that once a year, during the daffodil season, the head of the firm paid Cornwall a visit; and later on, between seasons, his representative. And it was his representative who arrived on that hot afternoon when Jeannie and I were despondent.

He was in a hurry. He had another appointment for which he was already late, and he said he knew we would understand. A brush off possibly, almost inevitably, if spoken by another kind of person. He knew we would understand, he said, because never from the beginning of the season to the end were there ever any complaints about our flowers. They ask for them specially, he said, and it is always a pleasure to open your boxes and show them.

'You give something to the flower trade, you two.'

I believe when he said this that both of us felt so emotional that we wanted forcibly to restrain him from leaving us. He had given us the key. He had made no deliberate effort to do so but his antennae, without which a talented person will be ordinary, had sensed we needed a lift. And we were able excitedly and so happily to respond. Here was an instant of good luck without which no endeavour can succeed; and the only issue at stake was taking advantage of it. The hot afternoon, after he had left, had to be made to work.

As soon as his car disappeared up the lane, we realized too where lay our friends; and although our connection with them might be by the tenuous communication of newly turned soil, daffodil bulbs, flowers, picking and bunching them, rushing them to the station, and awaiting the post for the envelope containing the prices, the world they lived in was indeed a real world.

We knew also that we must not betray all the struggle, sacrifice, and enthusiasm which led the way to us receiving such a compliment. We must attack. This collision between despondency and the praise we had received was a reflection of all the years we had been at Minack. The earth and the rain and the wind may have hurt us but they had never, I felt, dimmed the truth of our optimism. We struggled where we loved. Failure was in the hands of the gods, not in the hands of human beings. When we fought for our survival, we did not have to weary ourselves waiting upon the whims of other people. We were alone. We were together.

'Jeannie,' I said, such relief in my mind and the enthusiasm simmering again which had been curbed in the tight circle of wavering defeatism, 'let's give ourselves one more chance!'

'Oh yes, I agree.'

'I want to see Minack a show place of daffodils. I want to fight all those things which have been dulling our happiness.'

Jeannie was smiling at me.

'Don't get too fierce!'

'Oh I know I sound melodramatic, but that's how I feel. For better or for worse I want to slam them all!'

'You will.'

'And so I'm going to play a hunch. The only person I know who can help us to achieve what we want is Geoffrey. I saw his father the other day and it is just possible Geoffrey wants to return to Minack.'

'He loved the cliffs.'

'I'll write to him and ask him whether he will come and see us on Wednesday evening.'

Wednesday was the day after the morrow. It was also Fred's birthday.

XVIII

I was up early in the morning, a glorious, hazy, warm May morning, and went down to the rocks for a bathe. Fishing boats, a half mile offshore, were hurrying to Newlyn market and gulls swirled in their wake. Two cormorants on the other side of the little bay, black sentinels in the sunlight, were standing on a rock regally surveying the scene; and on my left, up in the woods of the cliff, wood pigeons cooed. The scent of the sea filled the air, crystals sparkled the water, and the sound of the lazy, lapping waves was like a chorus of ghosts telling the world to hush. No angry engines in the sky disturbed the peace of it. No roar of traffic dulled the senses. Here was the original freedom. Here was poised a fragment of time when the world was young.

When I returned to the cottage, Fred and Penny were standing in the field looking down into the garden, and Jeannie was at the door.

'We've been waiting for you,' she said, laughing, 'Fred's been getting impatient.'

He began to whimper, nostrils quivering, the prelude to a bellow. 'Hold it, Fred, hold it,' I called, 'we've got a present for you!' Then Jeannie went inside and brought back a huge bunch of carrots. 'Happy birthday!' we said, holding the bunch in front of him.

Fred, and Penny for that matter, was clearly surprised at such an array of carrots so early in the morning. They were even more surprised when ten minutes later two children's voices came singing round the corner; 'Happy birthday to you!' Susan and Janet from the farm at the top had arrived, like Cornish pixies, with their presents. More carrots! And it was not yet eight o'clock.

Fred, in a way, had become a mascot to the children of St Buryan parish in which we lived. They had been told of the days when donkeys clip-clopped the lanes of the district; and how the fishermen of Sennen Cove had the finest collection of donkeys in Cornwall, racing each other through St Buryan village on the way to Newlyn with their catches; but these seemed like fairy stories to those who had never seen a donkey. An old doctor on his rounds, before the first world war, was the last to be remembered using a donkey cart in St Buryan parish; but no one could remember when a donkey was last born. Fred, therefore, was a character of the imagination which had become real. His birthday, his first birthday, was an occasion. And the children were going to celebrate it.

Fred now had time to digest his early morning presents. There was a pause in his festivities and he roamed around the field flicking his tail and nibbling the grass, then suddenly appeared again to look down into the garden.

'Fred seems to be hinting at something,' said Jeannie.

I looked up at him. Fluffy brown coat, a brown pillow of a fringe between his two big ears and the white of his nose, a sturdy, slightly arched little back, the black cross easy to see, and a pair of intelligent eyes which were saying: 'She's right. I am!'

'Nothing doing, Fred,' I said, 'you must wait for the party this afternoon.'

At that moment I heard the postman singing his way down the lane on his bicycle. Part-time postman, cobbler, hairdresser, fish and chip merchant, he had a key part to play in the coming events. He also sold ice-creams. And he also always arrived at Minack happily smiling, whatever the gales, the rain or the snow.

'Lovely morning, Mr Gilbert,' I said.

'And a lovely morning for a donkey's birthday,' he replied. He began to search through his satchel. 'I've got something here I've never carried before. A telegram for a donkey! And there's a big envelope for Fred too. Birthday cards from the school.' He paused, still searching. 'Ah, here they are . . .' Then he added when he had handed them to me: 'I've seen the schoolmaster. Thirty-two will be coming from the school, and so what with the grown-ups I reckon forty cornets will see it through.'

'Leave it to you,' I said.

'I'll be down soon after half-past three.'

A telegram and, within the envelope, thirty-two birthday cards! We were under an obligation to play the game with respect. Much earnest thought and trouble had gone into the making of it. A ritual had to be observed. Whether Fred was personally interested or not, each greeting had to be read to him; and in any case Jeannie and I were exceedingly touched that the children should have remembered him.

'Many happy returns to Freddie. Love Sally and Linda,' said the telegram. How had they remembered the date? Two schoolgirls from London who had come to Minack as strangers to see if they could meet the gull on the roof; and then had spent the afternoon playing with Penny and Fred. I held the telegram up to him and he pushed his nose into it. 'Do you remember how Sally spent an hour grooming you and you loved it?'

There were carrots galore on the birthday cards. Each card had been individually drawn in coloured crayon, imaginative, primitive drawings, the figure one prominent in all of them, some with poems attached, cut-outs of other donkeys painstakingly pasted on thick paper, messages of good wishes in carefully written script, joke drawings like donkeys fishing ('I hope you catch your carrot.'), romantic drawings of a donkey ruminating in a pasture, another with ships as a background; all kindly and thoughtful and original. Something so much more important was there than the cards themselves, and we now awaited the arrival of those who sent them. And so did Fred.

When they came he could have been excused if he had been startled by their number. He had never seen so many children before, so many gay, shouting children who tumbled out of cars, running up the path to the field, calling: 'Happy birthday, Freddie!' This was a carnival of a party, a boy was dressed as the Mad Hatter, battered top hat and tails too big for him, another wore a huge mask of the March Hare, girls in party frocks with ribbons in their hair, boys chasing each other, all converging on Fred who stood his ground half-way up the slope of the field with ears pricked; and I would have forgiven him if he had turned and fled. Thirty-two children swarming towards him, screams of laughter, yells of glee, this cacophony of happiness made noise enough to·scare him into leaping into the next field. He did not budge. He awaited the onslaught of arms being flung around him, ears pulled, mane ruffled, nose kissed and kissed again, pats on the back, tail tugged, as if it were an experience to which he had long been accustomed. All through the afternoon he allowed himself to be treated as a toy, and not once did he show impatience. Dear one-year-old Fred. This was indeed his hour of glory.

There were rewards, of course. His guests, for instance, vied with each other in their generosity, eating part of their ice-cream cornets then pushing them towards a large, welcoming mouth. He had always loved ice-cream. And there were the sticky lollipops, the shape and colour of carrots which Jeannie had bought; and these too were dangled before him in such a way that when accepted, kudos was obtained.

Penny, meanwhile, was having her own passage of fame. Fred, being too young to carry anyone, Penny had to play the role of the patient beach donkey. Can I have a ride? Can I? Can I? Up and down the field she went, solemnly and safely. Sometimes two astride her back, sometimes even three. She plodded on in the manner of a donkey who knew how to earn its living. She waited quietly as someone was heaved upon her back, she moved on at the right moment, she halted as soon as a fair ride had been completed. Can I have a ride? Can I? Can I?

There they were, two donkeys with ice-cream smeared about their faces, sucking lollipops; Fred a toy donkey, Penny a working one, when the time came for The Cake. Jeannie had made it, a table on the field was ready for it, and there was a single candle.

The air was still, and with ceremony the candle was lit. The table was at the bottom of the field above the wood and so its shelter helped the flame to burn steadily and with no fear of it flickering out. All around were Fred's guests. There was chattering and laughter, and from somewhere in the background a small voice began the customary birthday song.

'Too soon!' someone else shouted.

Fred, at that moment, had not arrived. He was a few yards away in a cluster of admirers, a girl with golden hair holding the halter, and all of them edging Fred towards the climax of his party. He did not want to be rushed. He was going to arrive in his own good time. And suddenly the shouts went up: 'Here's Freddie! Happy birthday, Freddie! Good old Freddie!' Treble voices sailing into the sky. A moment in time that many years away, most would remember. Nothing complicated. The same pleasure that centuries have enjoyed.

Fred reached the table. The candle on the cake, a strong, confident flame, awaited him. But I do not think anyone who was present believed he would so successfully fulfil their secret hopes.

As the children sang his birthday song, Fred pushed his head forward inquiringly towards the candle, snorted; and blew it out.

The children had gone, Minack was quiet again, and we now awaited Geoffrey; and we soon saw him coming down the lane. There was a sense of continuity about the sight of him, as if it were one of those days years ago, when he worked at Minack; and it would have been easy had I shut my eyes, to believe that Shelagh was riding down the lane behind him on her bicycle, and that Jane too had arrived across the fields from her cottage above the cliffs she loved. These three who in a period of struggle for survival, had given us their loyalty and enthusiasm; and now that I saw him again, his presence drove a sharp awareness into my private world of doubts and frustrated plans that once again we could set about building upon the base of Minack.

In this impermanent world in which restlessness is a deception for contentment, in which the individual can only salvage what he can from the twilight pressures of the mass, in which to be sensitive is no longer a grace, in which haste without purpose, second-hand pleasures, package thinking and noise for the sake of it are the gods of millions; in which truth is an expendable virtue in the pursuit of power, and in which youth is compelled from the beginning to worship materialism, Jeannie and I could touch the old stones of Minack, brace ourselves before the gales, listen to the sea talking and to the gulls crying, be at one with the animals, have time to search our inward selves and fight the shadow which is the enemy; and to marvel at the magic which had led us to a life we loved so much.

'Do you realize,' said Jeannie, after Geoffrey, as enthusiastic as we had hoped him to be, had gone back up the lane and the date of his return had been agreed, 'that we now can go away as we planned a year ago?'

'I do.'

'And neither of us now want to?'

'Neither of us.'

'It seems to prove something.'

'What?'

Jeannie paused for a moment, leaning against a rock and staring out into the wide sweep of Mount's Bay.

'I suppose I mean,' she said, 'that if individuals are to be truly happy they should have a purpose in life which does not trample on others.'

'Only a few can have such an opportunity. The rest have to fight for a living in jobs they do not enjoy.'

'That's what I mean. We are one of the few . . . and we have realized it.'

'We have solved what we set out to solve a year ago.'

'Yes.'

The dying sun was beginning to touch the fields across the valley. The shadows of boulders were sharp. The pilchard fleet of Newlyn was busily setting out towards the Wolf Rock. A happy day. A soft breeze off the sea, curlews flying high and calling, a wood-pecker laughing.

'Let's go and see the donkeys,' I said.

We reached the field and saw no sign of them.

'That's funny, I hope I didn't leave the gate open.'

'Look there they are!' said Jeannie.

At the far end of the field beneath the distant hedge I saw Penny standing dozily upright. On the grass beside her lying outstretched was Fred sound asleep. A donkey who had had a party, enjoyed every minute of it, and was now exhausted.

We did not disturb them.

THE HEARTWARMING TRUE STORY
OF A VERY SPECIAL DOG
AND HER VERY SPECIAL OWNER

SHEILA HOCKEN

(Illus)

Everyone knows the inspiring story of Sheila Hocken and
her wonderful guide-dog Emma, and of the miracle
operation which enabled her to see for the first time in her
life.

Now, Sheila describes her life since the incredible moment
when she opened her eyes and saw the beautiful world we
all take for granted. With freshness and humour, Sheila
tells how each day brought new joys, new challenges and
new surprises.

Emma's life, too, has undergone dramatic changes. She was
no longer needed as a guide-dog but her retirement has
been far from idle. She is now a celebrity and receives her
own fan mail; she has made several television appearances;
she was Personality Dog of the Year at Crufts and is greeted
in the street more often than Sheila is.

'Writing simply, with innate ability to externalise thought,
feeling, experience, she again achieves a lovable intimacy'
Daily Telegraph

AUTOBIOGRAPHY 0 7221 4601 9 £1.25

Also by Sheila Hocken in Sphere Books:
EMMA AND I

By the Green of the Spring

JOHN MASTERS

1918 dawns desolate over the fields of Flanders. Decimated
by the worst war the world has ever seen, neither British
nor German troops can break the deadlock of the trenches.
After four years of murderous stalemate, peace seems buried
for ever. But finally, one by one, the guns fall silent . . .

BY THE GREEN OF THE SPRING

relives the last terrible months of the Great War and the
uneasy, exhausted peace which followed it.

BY THE GREEN OF THE SPRING

from the North-West Frontier to the war in France and the
civil war in Ireland, John Masters follows the fortunes of
four Kent families – the Cates, the Rowlands, the Strattons
and the Gorses – through the cataclysm that ended the
golden Edwardian dream for ever.

BY THE GREEN OF THE SPRING

is the third, self-contained volume of the **LOSS OF EDEN**
trilogy, a magnificent conclusion to an enthralling epic of
war and peace by a major contemporary novelist.

GENERAL FICTION   0 7221 0468 5   £2.50

A selection of bestsellers from SPHERE

FICTION

ONCE IN A LIFETIME	Danielle Steel	£1.95 □
WHALE	Jeremy Lucas	£1.75 □
THE NEXT	Bob Randall	£1.75 □
REALITIES	Marian Schwartz	£2.25 □
PACIFIC VORTEX!	Clive Cussler	£1.95 □

FILM & TV TIE-INS

WIDOWS	Lynda La Plante	£1.50 □
THE YEAR OF LIVING DANGEROUSLY	C. J. Koch	£1.50 □
E.T. THE EXTRA-TERRESTRIAL	William Kotzwinkle	£1.50 □
HONKYTONK MAN	Clancy Carlile	£1.95 □
INCUBUS	Ray Russell	£1.50 □

NON-FICTION

THE SINGLE FILE	Deanna Maclaren	£1.95 □
NELLA LAST'S WAR	Nella Last	£1.95 □
THE NUCLEAR BARONS	P. Pringle & J. Spigelman	£3.50 □
THE CONTAINED GARDEN	K. Beckett, D. Carr & D. Stevens	£6.95 □

All Sphere books are available at your local bookshop or newsagent, or can be ordered direct from the publisher. Just tick the titles you want and fill in the form below.

Name _____

Address _____

_____

Write to Sphere Books, Cash Sales Department, P.O. Box 11, Falmouth, Cornwall TR10 9EN

Please enclose a cheque or postal order to the value of the cover price plus:

UK: 45p for the first book, 20p for the second book and 14p for each additional book ordered to a maximum charge of £1.63.

OVERSEAS: 75p for the first book plus 21p per copy for each additional book.

BFPO & EIRE: 45p for the first book, 20p for the second book plus 14p per copy for the next 7 books, thereafter 8p per book.

Sphere Books reserve the right to show new retail prices on covers which may differ from those previously advertised in the text or elsewhere, and to increase postal rates in accordance with the PO.